Published by **Enete Enterprises**

1321 Upland Dr. Houston, TX 77043 (USA)

1st Edition of
Becoming an Expat
Costa Rica

Becoming an Expat Costa Rica 1st edition / Shannon Enete

Printed in the United States of America
www.EneteEnterprises.com

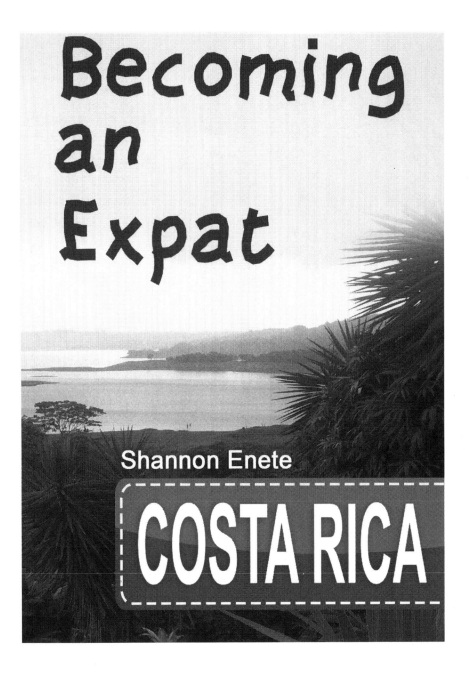

Becoming an Expat

Shannon Enete

COSTA RICA

OTHER BOOKS BY THIS AUTHOR

- ☑ Becoming an Expat Ecuador
- ☑ Becoming an Expat Thailand
- ☑ Becoming an Expat Mexico
- ☑ Becoming an Expat 101
- ☑ Becoming a Nomad
- ☑ Earn an Income Abroad
- ☑ Life Another Way: *become the best version of you from your favorite place on earth*
- ☑ Teeth Not Tears: Smiles Through the Rubble

visit: www.Becominganexpat.com for more information

"This is a fantastic reference! Thorough, with all of the information I needed to make the decision and complete my move abroad!"

~ Lisa, Virgina

"This book is a must have for anyone considering the move to Costa Rica. It's packed with real information unlike many of the other books that sell a dream. I learned the good and the bad."

~ Gina, California

For all of you who want to work to live and not live to work.

DEDICATION

To all of my expat friends who have shared their experiences and wisdom to shape this book with real life accuracy and a comprehensive experience. To my love who tolerates my marathon writing spurts.

TABLE OF CONTENTS

PART IV - Family & Education.............. 177

Moving with a Family

Testimonials

Acclimating the Children

PART V - Work & Business.................. 201

Work Hard Play Hard

INTRODUCTION

Costa Rica is a mesmerizing country peppered with cultural and natural treasures. That being said, it's not for everyone. There are those whose temperament are not patient enough for this slow moving land. This book is not intended to sell you on the move, instead, it was written to help you decide if Costa Rica is the right fit for you. Over the years expats have flooded to the tropical oasis resulting in a raise of the cost of living and a transformed atmosphere.

This material is a culmination of my experience and the experiences of numerous expats living in the *pura vida*. The words that follow are not sugar-coated like other international lifestyle resources that attempt to sell you a dream. Included is the good, the bad, the stuff in-between, and the stuff you would never have thought of. We're not selling real estate or harbor ulterior motives.

Costa Rica (CR) is the land of liberties, freedom, and nature. On the flip side of those liberties lye disorganization, latency, and inefficiency. The side that you choose to focus on will directly relate to your happiness and overall experience living in the *pura vida*, "pure life."

Keep an eye out for updates on www.BecominganExpat.com in-between editions since the ever-changing immigration laws, cost of living, and international experience evolves constantly.

If Costa Rica is one of many countries that you are weighing as your new home, check out our other editions: Ecuador, Mexico, Thailand, and 101 for those who just don't know where yet. We also have an Earn an Income Abroad book to help you finance your international life and a book designed to help you live life on your terms, passions, and dreams; Life Another Way.

PART I

THE BASICS

All of the essential information needed to get you up and
running towards or away from Costa Rica

THE BASICS

AN INTRODUCTION TO A NEW COUNTRY AND CULTURE

Costa Rica (CR) literally translates to "rich coast." Boasting the highest standards of living in Central America while maintaining a hippie-like democracy without an armed force. Instead of war, Costa Rica has allocated money towards the green revolution, health, and education. In the 19th century, coffee production paid the bills.

Today, while coffee, pineapples, bananas, palm oil, and other exports certainly add pennies in the bank, the real cash-cow is tourism.

HISTORY

Located in Central America, Costa Rica was a melting pot where Indians from the north intermixed with those from the south. Humans have walked along CR's jungles and beaches for over 10,000 years with signs of Aztec, Mayan, and Huetar Indian influences.

Christopher Columbus shook things up when he made an unplanned visit in 1502 after a hurricane damaged his ship. His vessel limped into the Caribbean Coast near modern day's Puerto Limón. While the ship underwent repairs, Chris decided to take a stroll. He claimed later to the Queen to have seen exorbitant amounts of gold. His letters describing 'la costa rica' seemed to have dubbed the country's name.

It took almost 60 years of battles and biological warfare before the first Spanish colony was established. Columbus and his army of Spaniards were more concerned about conquering rather than preserving, which combined with intense storms, resulted in the loss of much of the ancient history.

Preservation was not the only thing handled loosely. Since Central America was so far away from its new *"owner"* Spain, there was more leniency in governance. The nearest military post was in Guatemala.

That distance paved the way for the development of a new class that operated outside of the slave-driven model, the self-sufficient farmer. This class became the backbone for rural democracy, but not without a fight.

After Mexico emancipated itself from Spain, it seemed as if the empire was a free-for-all. A civil war broke out between the conservatives of Cartago who preferred a colonial administration versus the San José liberals who favored a constitutional republic and progress. When the liberals prevailed in 1823, they moved the capital to their home town where it remains today.

The only major-archaeological site discovered to date is located in CR's Central Valley in a town called Guayabo.

CONSERVATION

Over the last 50 years, Costa Ricans have taken large steps to preserve their country. In 1963, Costa Rica created the first protected park, *Reserva Natural Absoluta Cabo Blanco*. At the time of this writing, Costa Rica maintains 27 national parks, 58 wildlife refuges, 32 protected zones, 15 wetland areas, 11 forest reserves, 8 biological reserves, and 12 other conservation regions equalling a staggering 25% of the country!

CR reasoned that with the fluctuation of import/ export prices the best thing to import would be tourists, and import them they did! In 2015 over 2.66 million people visited the country shattering previous records! $2.882 BILLION dollars were introduced into the tiny country's economy!

They are learning a balance between tourism and conserving their precious eco-system. They are pioneers in conservation, recognizing that the best way to maintain a healthy tourism industry was to protect the nature that tourists seek.

STABILITY

Two presidents ago, Oscar Arias, won the Nobel Peace Prize, received the Albert Schweitzer Prize for Humanitarianism, and served as a trustee of Economists for Peace and Security! How is that for stable? In his Noble Peace Prize acceptance speech, he shared some of his ideals, *"We seek peace and democracy together, indivisible, an end to the shedding of human blood which is inseparable from an end to the suppression of human rights."* He sounds more like Dali Lama than a president, which to this author is a breath of fresh air. Laura Chinchilla was elected to office in 2009 as CR's first female president, and the current president, Luis Guillermo Solís, took office in 2014.

CR's constitution clearly defines the nation as Roman Catholic but simultaneously guarantees freedom of religion. As of the 2011 census CR is:

70.5% Roman Catholic

44.9% practicing Catholics 13.8% Protestant

11.3% without religion

04.3% other religions

MILITARY

What military? That's right, CR does not employ an armed force! Not since Dec 1st of 1948. President José Figueres Ferrer abolished the military after the civil war victory. A year later, article 12 of the constitution was added making the disarming of the country permanent. The funding previously allocated for the military is now used in education and healthcare which is strikingly different from the United States policies.

"Feliz la madre costarricense que sabe al parir que su hijo nunca será soldado"

"It's a happy Costa Rican mother who gives birth knowing her child will never be a soldier"
                              ~ Ryoichi Sasakawa
For those who take stock in residing in a country that can deploy nuclear warheads, this news might be unsettling.

CRIME

Crime varies in CR just like it does everywhere in the world. Larger cities encounter big crime. San José and Limón have the highest occurrence both violent and petty. The most common problem is petty theft. So by leaving that expensive SLR camera in the back seat of your rental car you can consider it and your window a donation.

On occasion, rental cars are targeted. It has been reported that thieves have punctured tires on rental cars, then followed the driver until they pull over to fix the flat. The thieves then arrive as if they're good samaritans offering assistance. The only assistance they actually provide is lightening your load by removing all your possessions, and potentially the rental car. I have never experienced this, nor know anyone that has but am aware it happens and now so are you.

Don't place a personal bag above you on the bus. It is very easily lifted by someone else exiting the bus before you, possibly without your knowledge until it's too late.

Violent crimes are not as common here. There has never been a mass murder, no school shootings, and no issues with terrorism. For more on crime, see the United States Department of State OSAC Bureau of Diplomatic Security website: www.osac.gov/Pages/ContentReportDetails.aspx?cid=12155

To provide some perspective, I am from San Diego and consider most places in Costa Rica to be safer outside of one big factor. I don't feel comfortable displaying expensive gadgets. For example, I usually don't bring my 15" MacBook Pro out of my house as I would in the States. In San Diego, I carried it and often worked from Panera or Starbucks. In CR, I keep it for working at home. The value of that MacBook in Costa Rica is 1.5 times the value of it in the States. Minimum wage for many Ticos is $450 a month. That makes my laptop very enticing to the wrong person. They could feed their family for months! This was a small inconvenience for me, but well worth the trade off of living in Costa Rica. I do see other people display their computers. Call me paranoid, but I wouldn't recommend it.

SEX

Latin America is known for having beautiful men and woman and the sex appeal is never lacking. In fact, sex is a legal business. Prostitution is regulated and legal. Prostitutes must be at least 18 years of age and disease free. They carry ID cards from the health department (carnets de salud) that deem them clean from STDs. Not all prostitutes keep their cards up to date, nor does having an up to date card actually translate to being disease free. The HIV virus can take up to 6 month to produce a positive test. There are numerous bars and brothels in and around San José, Jaco, Tamarindo, and other nightlife driven locations. The age for consensual sex in Costa Rica is 16.

Underage prostitution, or sex exploitation is a huge problem in Costa Rica. The government is aware of the problem and since has formed the Commission Against the Sexual Exploitation of Children in the attempt to halt sex tourism and trafficking. You may also notice a poster in an airport or government office warning against under-age sex tourism. However, their efforts have not seemed to turn around the trend. INTERPOL has named Costa Rica as the country soon to become the sex tourism capital of its hemisphere.

As far as STDs go, surprisingly Costa Rica is not a standout for contraction of diseases. Possibly due to the ID cards and legal regulation of prostitution. The occurrence of STDs in Costa Rica is comparable to those found in France, Italy, and Canada according to the CIA fact book.

ECONOMY

Costa Rica has the strongest and most robust economy in Central America and continues to grow. As of the writing of this book, the population was over 4.76 million people with a growth rate of 1.5% annually. Since expats have flocked to Costa Rica to retire in paradise, real estate prices have slowly crept higher. Other items, such as cheese, fuel, and utilities have also climbed. A pizza is downright expensive!

If you ask an expat who has lived in CR for more than 5 years, they will call CR pricey, and are often bitter about the increase in living expenses. However, expense is all about perspective. If you move from midwest America, then you may find it to be comparable, if you are from Southern California, then you'll think it's a steal! My advice to you is compare our budgets and spending to your current cost of living and see what you get for your dollar or Colón, then decide if it is a steal or a rip off. Read more in the **Cost of Living** section.

CULTURE

CR's slogan, "Pura Vida," is an excellent representation of life in the idyllic country. It literally translates to 'pure life' and is used as a greeting, declaration, and salutation. You will hear, experience, and see *pura vida* everywhere you go.

Ticos model how to live pura vida in every aspect of their lives. They are gentle, kind people who rush for no one. They place family and human connection above aspiration and materialistic objects. They strive to please you to a fault. For example, if you need your car repaired by the next day, your mechanic might assure it's no problem when it is not likely possible at all. This is not because they want to deceive you or suck more money from you. They only strive to gain your approval, avoid disappointment, are eternal optimists, and avoid confrontation like the plague.   Keep this in mind if, or more realistically when, you become frustrated. After all, what's the hurry? You're in pura vida living on "Tico time."

As a Roman Catholic nation, the culture is a culmination of old fashioned ideals intertwined with catholicism. When you ask a pico "How are you? Como estas? A common response is "Bien, gracias a

Dios," which translates to, "Good, thanks be to God." Many Ticos don't believe in the use of birth control and abortion is illegal. Small towns are deserted on Sundays and divorce is frowned on even though occurrences are on the rise.

Many traditions are alive and well in CR. Particularly those rooted from the country's heavy agricultural past. Ox carts, also called *las carretas*, provide an excellent example. The carts exude an important symbol of pride and culture for Ticos. They were originally pulled by people, providing the only source of transportation. In the 1840's, the demand for coffee exploded which created immensely heavy loads. That's when the oxen entered the scene. In order to differentiate plantation families the carts were hand painted.

Today you will observe a combination of oxen and tractors pulling larger carts. No matter how many times you see the oxen, it's nearly impossible to become jaded. Their majesty, massive presence, elegant headwear, and historical significance continues to impress.

The carts are proudly displayed in parades and historical sites. The largest display is held annually in Escazú on the second Sunday in March. Tourist shops capitalize on the carts popularity, selling thousands of miniature versions as souvenir magnets or keepsakes each year.

Costa Rica is one of the most literate nations in the world at 96.3%! Costa Rica was one of the first countries in Latin America to offer a free and mandatory education for all children. Since CR has become a popular expat destination, numerous private schools have popped up around the nation that offer topnotch bilingual education geared for international students. Read more about children and schools in the **Education** section.

GAY / LESBIAN

While Costa Rica does not fly a rainbow flag nor recognize same sex marriages, they are fairly tolerant of the LGBT community. Latin women are often seen holding hands or linking arms so lesbians can often blend in with the accepted norm. I am a proudly out and have encountered zero hostility. My next door neighbors are also a lesbian couple!

The only hitch that I encountered was being told by a hotel staff member that public displays of affection were not allowed because Costa Rica was a traditional country and a guest complained. After speaking with the extremely apologetic hotel manager, I was assured that the staff would be retrained, my meals were comped, and we were offered a free night stay. He insisted that they were gay friendly, and had just hosted a gay marriage the previous weekend.

Costa Rica is no less hospitable than the United States. In fact, I would argue that it may be more peaceful for gays here than many parts of the US. I often attract perplexed or curious looks but that could be due to the fact that I'm a 6'0'' tall woman with short hair in a country filled with tiny women. I usually smile and make conversation with the curious onlookers, and they almost always supply a cheerful response.

Small towns see very few openly gay Costa Ricans, however, San José is host to a handful of gay hot spots. Men can expect a few more challenges in small towns due to the expectation of machismo behavior.[1]

I have met a handful of other lesbian and gay expats that happily live in Costa Rica.

---

[1] aggressive male behavior expected in latin american culture

WATER

The water in CR is safe for drinking in most areas. Hurray! No need to brush your teeth with bottled water! Even though it's safe to drink, it is always wise to allow your body to adjust to the new foods, bacterias, and minerals. Also, do some investigating of your own in your community to assure the safety of the water filtration system.

I purchased a 20 gallon water jug (designed to work with a cooler or dispenser) for about $5.00 USD and used it for my home water needs. When I dine out, I order "Agua de la casa" or tap water. The reason I purchase water for home use is because I've read that the water in CR is high in calcium and thus could potentially increase the likelihood of kidney stones. The validity of this is completely unknown to me. Also, in the community where I reside, clay commonly infiltrates the water supply. While Costa Rican clay is beautiful, in my water or GI tract it's less than desirable.

FOOD

Costa Rican food leaves you feeling fulfilled, light, and ready for the adrenaline packed activities that CR is known for. The foods boast mild flavors and is rarely processed. The produce is second to none!

The national dish of CR is gallo pinto which consists of rice and black beans sautéed together with a variety of veggies. Gallo pinto is served for breakfast alongside a piece of locally made cheese and a fried egg. The typical Costa Rican dish is called a casado which is a creative name since the same word means married. They marry the best foods to create a well balanced dish of rice, beans, a vegetable medley, small green salad, plantain, and choice of pork, fish, red meat, or chicken.

Costa Rica is home of some of the best fruit in the world. Picture mangos dangling on the massive trees encased in a warm blanket of tropical sun and salt water infused air. No wonder they turn out so sweet. No greenhouse or chemicals needed.

To wet your whistle, there are a variety of options! For breakfast sip on world famous locally grown coffee alongside of refrescos naturales *(homemade juices)*: guanabana, passion fruit, tamarind, mango, and more. Orange juice will never be your only option in Costa Rica!

When the warm sun has parched your lips, stroll over to the nearest bar or restaurant for an Imperial, Pilsner, or Bavaria beer. These three are the best Costa Rican brewed beers. Imperial is by far the most popular and is ideal for those wheat/light beer lovers. Pilsner is the second most popular and a bit more bitter for those that are looking for a little bite. Lastly, Bavaria is a fuller bodied beer and also the only dark beer option brewed in CR.

LANGUAGE

If your native tongue is anything other than Spanish, the above mentioned alcohol might be needed to help loosen your tongue to converse with the locals. It is true, Costa Ricans do indeed speak Spanish.

While there is some English spoken in touristy areas such as: Tamarindo, Montezuma, Jaco, Monteverde, Playa Flaminco, and Arenal, your stay will be infinitely more enjoyable and doable if you learn Spanish.

English is taught as the second language in the public school system, but currently about 11% of Ticos speak some English. As an expat, if want to experience the tico way of life language skills are a must!

The Caribbean Coast is it's own beast. The Jamaican descendants brought with them an English based creole called Mekaytelyuw; otherwise known as patois or pidgin. This is one of the many obvious standouts about CR's Caribbean Coast.

CLIMATE

Costa Rica's climate varies from beautiful to jaw-dropping gorgeous. You can choose to live in the valley and experience 72 degrees year round or venture into the depths of the jungle amongst the sloths and enjoy 80s year round. If you'd rather slip on flip flops and cruise the beach, you can expect to bask under a 95 degree sun with the coconuts and McCaws. If you enjoy crisp air, there are options for you in the higher elevations where you can experience autumn-like temperatures year round! Finally, if your friends tell you that you are always in the clouds, then you might want to choose to live in them literally in the damp majestic cloud forest!

There are two seasons in CR, wet and dry. The wet, or rainy, season is dubbed such because it is the time of year when CR gets most of the rainfall required to maintain that mind-blowing green landscape! In most of the country *(excluding the Caribbean)* the wet season is from May through November. In these seven months, CR receives an average of 40-240 inches *(101-610cm)* of rain dependent on the location. The northeast region receives the most rain and the northwest region the least (See: http://costa-rica-guide.com/Weather/WeatherMap.html for rainfall in the region you are interested in living). During this time, the rain changes in intensity. In May-June, it mostly rains at night providing an excellent sound track to snooze to, not to mention some epic lighting shows. Picture palm trees silhouetted by lightning bolts!

Then July-Sept it rains for an hour or two during the mid to late afternoon and again all night. Still, the rain is not yet interfering greatly with everyday life. By the end of September and through November, the rain picks up drastically often raining the entire day.

The above descriptions are accurate depictions for the Central Pacific Coast. Check the weather map for each region to be certain you are prepared for the rainfall that your area will endure. Guanacaste is the driest region and therefore does not have many days of full rain. The North Caribbean Coast is the wettest region with heavy rainfalls often commencing in July.

I visited Tortuguero in July, and the entire village flooded. Since the village is smack between mangroves, wetlands, and the Caribbean Sea, there wasn't many places for water to go but pool up together. In a very small amount of time, I found myself walking in two feet of standing water. So I found a boat tied to a tree with a "captain" willing to evacuate me and a few other backpackers to Limón for a fee.

Most locals and expats favor the wet season over the dry season for numerous reasons:

- Green landscapes are the most vibrant
- Rainfalls are refreshing and do not cause a chill
- Temperatures are slightly less oppressive
- Tourist's low season so there are less people to share paradise with

My personal favorite time of year is May-July.

NATURE

The 500,000 species roaming around the country make CR a stand out hosting 4% of the entire world's biodiversity. There are over 300,000 species of extraordinary insects like the silver beetle, mammals including the adored sloth, puma, rare and deadly amphibians, slithering reptiles, and a plethora of swimming creatures! The diversity of life in CR is what makes the *pura vida.*

The country's location between North and South America lends itself as a host to an emergence of life. Costa Rica possesses the highest *density* of biodiversity in the world.

TRANSPORTATION

Public transportation is ample in all parts of Costa Rica. Whether you are looking to go to the airport or the market, there is a bus or multiple buses that will get you there. Taxis are also available in all major cities and are usually available in smaller cities by telephone request.

That being said, you must decide if public transit is for you or are you more accustomed to the freedoms that owning your own automobile provides.

I moved to CR with the idea that I would use a combination of public transit and my own two feet to get from point A to point B. Within two weeks of moving to CR, I started shopping for a vehicle.

Admittedly, I moved to a small pueblo in the Central Pacific Coast that did not have a lot of amenities within foot reach. I'm also very social and wanted the option to meet people for dinner or other occasions in nearby cities. The local buses in smaller towns stop service around 8pm which would not accommodate the lifestyle that I desired.

BUS EXPERIENCE

The buses are designed for a person statured 5'6'' or less, US children sized individuals, or adults that are about 5'4'' *(most Ticos I observe are between 5'0''-5'5'')*. If you are lengthier, then you can expect to be a bit cramped. Expect less legroom than most airline seats.

Depending on your location and time of day, the buses are susceptible to overcrowding and standing may be your only option. Women and the elderly get priority seating. If you see one standing, it is proper to give up your seat.

Standing can be inconvenient if your bus outing was to the grocery store. Leaning in the aisle with your groceries in tow is difficult but not impossible. Overcrowding only occurs in the busier cities and usually only during rush hour.

If you board hungry or thirsty, not to worry, venders often hop aboard and offer sweet and salty snacks or beverages for a few hundred colones.

Most local buses cost between 100-200 colones ($0.20-0.40 US) and arrive within 10 minutes of their schedule (http://www.visitcostarica.com/ict/paginas/LEYES/pdf/ ItinerarioBuses_en.pdf) Make sure to arrive 10-15 minutes early to the appropriate stop to assure that you don't miss your bus.

Take care of your belongings while on the bus. While I have not seen or experienced any trouble, I have read cautions and have friends who have items stolen when they placed their belongings above them in the overhead compartments. Keep your belongings on your lap or in-between your legs.

OWNING A VEHICLE

I have always preferred the freedom that having a set of wheels provides, but there are special considerations abroad. Purchasing a vehicle has a few extra hoops to jump through in CR. After you successfully purchase your car, knowing what to do if it breaks down is another story. Talking to a mechanic in Spanish, taking care of preventative maintenance, renewing Marchamo and Riteve are all things that you will encounter as a vehicle owner in Costa Rica. See the *Once You Have Arrived* section for more information.

DRIVING IN COSTA RICA

Driving in CR is not for the faint of heart. If you are timid or become overly stressed with a variety of driving conditions, this might not be the option for you. In one outing, you may encounter and navigate around tractors, oxen, horses, and other speedy drivers. Passing slower traffic by opposing traffic is an everyday occurrence. Nights in the wet season are host to torrential downpours and with little to no street lights, it creates a challenging driving environment. One night I not only had to navigate through the rain but around a massive horse running down the street!

Many residents opt out of driving at night because of the increase in difficulty and danger. With the Costa Rican pace and based on your personality that choice might not even cause an inconvenience.

Tico drivers are "free-spirited" meaning they treat rules as a guideline and do not necessarily adhere to them. While there are police enforcing driving regulations, they are not often found in the smaller towns so people drive as they like.

If you're hit with a speeding ticket, the penalties are steep! Costa Rica has the highest traffic fines in the Americas! *Starting* at $450US. If you are caught driving over 150Km/hr (95mph) you could spend a year in PRISON! I've never heard of that happening but the law is in the books. Turning right on a red light is illegal in CR and will cost you the same fine. It's not a huge problem because there are very few lights in Costa Rica, outside of the larger cities. I lived 45 minutes away from the nearest traffic signal. If you find yourself in San José, make sure that you are not driving on a "restricted day." Due to overcrowding, the city has placed a no drive rule according to the last number on your license plate, or *placa*. For example, if the last digit on your plate is a 1 or 2 then you cannot drive on Monday, 3 or 4 on Tuesday, 5 or 6 on Wednesday, 7 or 8 on Thursday, and 9 or 0 on Friday. The restriction is only effective during rush hour from 6:00am-8:30am and again from 4:30-7:00pm. The restriction does not apply to motorcycles, taxis, buses, and people with disabilities. The penalty for breaking the driving restriction is much more mild coming in at about $10US. http://www.autorent.cr/trafficfines/ I only mention the above to inform you, not to scare you. I have driven in Costa Rica with no problems and almost never see a patrol. When I do see an officer, he is usually standing on the side of the road looking to see if your Marchamo and Riteve are current (the equivalent to registration and vehicle safety inspection).[2] If you plan on living in an urban city however, you may encounter many more enforcement officials.

Other common differences between driving in the US and CR are that roads are often not clearly marked, not illuminated, and your GPS might not work. I have happily utilized the Google Maps App on my iPhone exclusively for my navigational needs; cellular service is required. Read more about cellular services in **Once You Have Arrived.**

IDENTIFICATION

It is highly recommended that you carry a copy of your passport and valid stamp on your person at all times. It doesn't sound practical but is required. Thankfully, expats before us have mastered the process.

There are numerous stores that offer *"copias"* or copies and lamination services. They can create a copy of your passport picture and shrink it to a standard card size. Then they copy the most recent entrance stamp on the back of the created card. Finally, they laminate the card, giving you a plastic waterproof card that is portable and easy to carry in your board shorts or wallet.If you are pulled over without this ID, you could find yourself in some trouble. I was pulled over once at a security check point, and I did not have the passport copy on me. I just rattled off my passport number which satisfied the officer, but I was lucky. Had I been pulled over for doing something errant, I believe my luck would not have been the same.

---

[2] More information about Reteve & Marchamo in "Once You Have Arrived"

IMMIGRATION

MANY ARE THE PATHS TO COSTA RICA. LEARN WHICH ROUTE IS BEST FOR YOU

Flocks of Americans, Canadians, Australians, and Europeans are migrating to CR and for good reason. The climate is luxurious, the people are welcoming, the pace relaxed, and nature abounds. Your love for the region could change after the glow of the honeymoon period wears off (read more about the phases you will experience in the *Culture Shock* section).

There are very few Costa Ricans leaving the country. Costa Rica's emigration is one of the lowest in the Caribbean Basin. Less than 3% of native Ticos live abroad. In 2005, there were 127,061 Costa Ricans living abroad as immigrants. Compare that to the United States' 3 - 6 Million.[3]

Conversely, Costa Rica's immigration is among the largest in the Caribbean Basin. Immigrants represent about 10.2% of the Costa Rican

---

[3] The number varies greatly because there is no reliable figure. The figure listed is the State Department's best estimate.

population. Most immigrants are from Nicaragua, Colombia, United States and El Salvador.

There are a variety of ways to migrate to CR but not everyone qualifies. Those who do not qualify usually opt for the popular perpetual tourist route.

PERPETUAL TOURIST

A perpetual tourist is someone who lives in Costa Rica but does not file for a Cedula, or Residency. So they enter the country on a 90 day tourist visa. Since they certainly intend on staying past their visa expiration they must journey to the border every 90 days to exit and re-enter. Thereby renewing their tourist visa. They can repeat this process indefinitely. This procedure has been practiced for over 20 years.

Rules are changing everyday and Costa Rican officials are hit and miss with enforcement of new regulations. There is no way of knowing if this way of life will remain possible indefinitely. Regulations are slowly popping up that exclude non-residents. For example, it was possible to obtain a CR drivers license without proof of residency. That changed in 2014.[4] In the past, perpetual tourists were allowed to purchase insurance through CAJA but no longer. It is best to be well informed and prepared. One of the newer requirements is showing proof of exit within your visa's timeframe.

For example, if you are entering Costa Rica on 1/1/14, then you must present a bus or plane ticket exiting the country no later than 3/31/14. Some agents are now turning you away if you just have a bus ticket. You can and very likely will be asked for this proof at the border crossing (Nicaragua & Panama) or even at the ticketing counter at the airport in the US.

---

[4] Read more about drivers license and driving requirements in **Once You Have Arrived**

Airline companies can be fined by Costa Rican Immigration for not viewing return documents before allowing the customer to proceed to the gate. In the case of deportation, the airline company could be charged the fee of transfer for the offending party to be returned back to their country of affiliation. If you plan on booking a one way ticket to Costa Rica from the US, make sure to have a ticket showing your exit out of Costa Rica.

A fellow expat, Rona Marino, was stuck in the US an additional week because she arrived at the airport without said proof. She was advised to either purchase a return ticket or return later with the required documentation.

There are a variety of ways to provide the required documentation, especially if you are creative on the computer. You could plan a small vacation every 90 days, and purchase bus or plane tickets for each trip ahead of time. Or you can do what many people do and buy a bus ticket at the border 80-90 days in advance.

Across the internet, and peppered throughout guidebooks is the rule, *"You must stay out of the country for 72 before re-admittance."* I am happy to inform you that rule is 100% inaccurate. It is only required to leave the country as long as it takes to: acquire the appropriate exit stamp, acquire an entrance stamp into a bordering town (Panama or Nico), then turn around to cross back into CR and obtain a new 90 day visa. I've done the entire procedure it in less than 20 minutes before.

PROOF OF FINANCIAL MEANS
In addition to proof of exit, border officials often ask to see a Credit Card with the Visa or MasterCard logo (platinum card is best). Or a wad of cash you can flash to show you are financially stable enough to enter the country, provide for yourself, and exit without a problem. *(This*

occurs most often at the pedestrian border crossings and less frequent at airport immigration.)

Border officials are not created equal. It is possible that during one of your border crossings the border official does not ask for any proof of exit or proof of financial means and grants you the desired 90 day visa. It is also possible that the next time your border official asks for proof of exit, and proof of financial means, he may decide to grant only a 60 day visa.

Beginning April 23rd, 2013, a new fine *(multa)* was put in place if you overstay your visa. $100USD for each month a tourist, or perpetual tourist, overstays his/her visa. Maintaining your visa is also important while driving on an international license. Once your tourist visa expires, you will be driving illegally and can be hit with a hefty fine.[5]

Filing for residency is the best method for longterm stays. It is possible to accomplish without an attorney but all documents must be translated into Spanish and the laws, forms, and bureaucracy is very confusing.

THE ABC's OF RESIDENCY

Below are the most popular ways to your cedula (residency card).

- **Pensionado** - *pension retirement of at least $12,000 per year*
- **Rentista** - *proof of $2,500 p/mo income for the last two years, or $60,000 deposited to a CR bank*
- **Investor** - *make an investment of $200,000 in a business or property*
- **Representante** - Be a *director of a company hiring a minimum number of local workers and other requirements*
- **Permanent** - *first degree relative, or after 3 years in one of the above categories*

---

[5] Read more about drivers license and driving requirements in **Once You Have Arrived**

RESIDENCY 101+

Immigration is a very complex topic which is why I advise you to get help. That being said, self-education is a great way to save time and learn to ask the right questions. This section dives deeper into each category including requirements, paperwork, and stipulations. If you are a "not into the details" kinda person and would rather leave that up to the pros then go ahead and skip forward to the next chapter.

Pensionado & Rentista

These are the most popular routes to residency. A Pensionado is someone who is collecting a public or private pension totaling over 12k per year. You qualify if your US retirement pension and/or Social Security payments collectively make the minimum $1,000 per month, or if you have other private pensions or annuities that will pay out the rest of your life which is equal to or greater than the magic number.

To qualify for Rentista, you must show proof of income greater than or equal to $2500 a month for over two years **or** make a deposit of $60,000 into a Costa Rican bank. Below you will see a variety of required documents and caveats:

💡Income must be re-proven at each renewal for Pensionado & Rentista until you become *Permanent.*

💡You must remain in Costa Rica for a minimum of 4 months each year.

💡Renew your residency identification card *(carnet or cedula)* every two years with a $100 fee per card.

💡Under Pensionado, you and your dependents cannot earn a salary. You can own and operate a business to pay yourself or make investments

Each Pensionado & Rentista must submit proof of income and proof of presence in CR for four months of the year each year to the Costa Rican government.

You are able to claim dependents under 18 years of age and your spouse in both categories without showing an increase in finances.

Specialized Documents Needed

- **Income Certificate**- proof of a pension of at least $1,000 p/mo stating that it is for life and will be paid in Costa Rica. Valid for 6 months. For for the Rentista, proof of income greater than or equal to $2500 a month for at least 2 years.

Residente Inversionista -Investor

Popularly dubbed "Buying your way in" the investor route is doing just that. Drop $200k in a business or property and you are on your way to becoming a resident. You could invest or start up a tourism business, fund a reforestation project, start a B&B, or purchase your dream home. The $200K can also be derived from a combination of vehicles and properties. So if you want to buy a sweet ride and a hideaway or rental property, you are well on your way to residency!

A draw back to the investor route is that no dependents can be included in this category. You also must reside in the country at least 6 months out of the year, tacking on 2 additional months over the Rentistas and Pensionados.

On the flip side, you are allowed to build income on your investments in Costa Rica in addition to owning and receiving dividends on a company.

Permanent

After three years as a Pensianado or Rentista, the resident is eligible to apply for permanent residency whereafter they will not be required to show financial statements and are only required to enter the county once a year to maintain residency.

First Degree Relative

You are granted permanent citizenship if you have a spouse, parent, brother, sister, or child that is a Costa Rican citizen, and they are willing to sponsor your application. You will be asked to prove relationship and financial ability to support yourself. This also applies to family members of foreigners who have become Costa Rican citizens.

Marriage

Marrying a Tico or Tica *(Costa Rican)* is the express lane to residency. This is the only category where you do not have furnish proof of a foreign income. It is also reportedly the fastest process. The take home message? When in doubt, fall in love! There is a catch. Due to abuse of this route, the new spouse does not receive permanent residency immediately, instead he/she has to wait 3 years while reapplying for temporary residency each year with her/his spouse in tow to prove their relationship is not a hoax.

Representante

This is a new path for immigration satisfying a growing population of international businesses entering Costa Rica and employing Ticos.

If you own or direct a company, *sociedad anónima,* and are able to prove that you satisfy a minimum number of employees, plus provide financial statements to back it up, you may qualify for residency. The downside is your spouse or dependents would not qualify. This residency requires renewal each year. You may apply for permanent residency after 3 years.

Residency Under Special Circumstances

To be eloquent, this option is a bit of a crap-shoot. Two identical applications with the exact same extenuating circumstances could be submitted and one may be approved and the other denied in true Tico fashion. Consult an attorney to find out if your circumstance holds water.

Temporary Residency - *Residencia Temporal*

Temporary Residency is a common route for students enrolled in a college or language school, peace corp volunteers and other secular and non-secular volunteer groups, employees of international companies, and language teachers. This residency is only valid for 3months to 1 year and can be renewed. Because this route is privy to a variety of situations, the paperwork is complex and extensive. You would be best suited to consult an attorney to facilitate the process. Once the mound of papers are completed and submitted, the turn around time is very quick.

If you have a shady past, you could be excluded from residency. Below is a list of crimes that automatically exclude you:

- Murder
- Drug or human trafficking
- Weapons or explosives trafficking
- Sexual crimes against minors, the elderly or the disabled
- Domestic violence
- Membership in designated gangs or in organized crime

IMMIGRATION WITH CHILDREN

When you have kids who are either residents or citizens *(born in Costa Rica)* you are not permitted to leave the country with them until they aquire their *permissions.* This requires a trip to La Uruca in San José. Make sure to take their cedulas, birth certificates, and passports with you to the main immigration office. Jessica and Chris learned this lesson the hard way when they attempted to fly back to Florida to visit family and friends with their four children. They were turned away and not permitted to check in for their flight.

When applying for their permissions you have a few options. You can opt to allow the children to fly with each parent solo, only fly when both parents are present, or only fly with one of the parents. Then at age 14 you can add permissions that allow the child to travel alone if that is your desire. Keep in mind that if you opt for the permissions requiring both parents to be present in order to leave the country if something happens to one parent you would not be permitted to leave before the permissions were changed.

WHERE DO YOU START?

As you see above, there is a LOT to immigration. It's also something you don't want to get wrong. Is it possible to file without a service? Yes, but I would not recommend it. The time, process, and headaches that you will save are well worth a quality attorney's fee. The average service fee ranges from $600-1200 USD.

Immigration services such as those offered by ARCR will translate all of your documents, provide access to their legal team, walk you through the process step by step, and answer your questions along the way. They will supply a check list to organize your process and will do for you what they have already done for thousands of expats before you, get you your cedula card!

TIP

Costa Rica LOVES paperwork and stamps, so just get used to it. Even at the hardware store they stamp the back of the receipt, staple, and stamp it again before it is finally handed to you.

Whether or not you opt to use a service, the starting point of the process is procuring documents from your country of origin and writing a letter announcing your intent to immigrate to CR. Below are the documents to get started on:

- ☐ A letter addressed to the head of immigration with: the reasons you are applying for residency, complete name, nationality, profession (if applicable), name and nationality of your parents, an email address to receive notifications from the Immigration Department, date, and signature.

- ☐ Birth certificate of the applicant, notarized and certified by the consulate in the applicant's home country then stamped by the foreign ministry in Costa Rica.

- ☐ A good girl/boy letter from the local police department in the applicants' home country certifying no criminal record in the last three years, notarized then certified by the home country government and the local consulate, and finally stamped by the foreign ministry in Costa Rica.

- ☐ Fingerprints from the Public Security Ministry in Desamparados.

- ☐ 3 recent passport-sized photos.

- ☐ A certified photocopy of all the pages in your passport

- ☐ Certification of registration with your home embassy.

- ☐ Apply for the CCSS Public Healthcare program otherwise called CAJA. Provide receipt proving the applicant has applied for CAJA.

☐A bank receipt for the application fee, *at time of writing it was $50 US if done from your home country, $250 if performed while in CR.*

☐A bank receipt for change of immigration category fee

☐All documents that are in any language other than Spanish must come with a translation completed by an *official translator.*

★All of the documents obtained in the United States MUST be notarized by a local notary if they do not have a government seal. They must then pass through the Secretary of State (for US) to be Apostilled. Then they must be authenticated by the Costa Rican consulate in the country where the document originated for $40 USD per document requiring authentication.

★After all of your documents have been prepared, translated, notarized, apostilled, and authenticated... phew... Then, fork over another $100 for the application fee and sit back and relax for the next 6 months to a year for processing.

★During the waiting period, you are permitted to stay in the country until a decision has been granted. You can also leave the country and return if so desired. I have known one person who did this and encountered some trouble reentering CR. His Immigration agent was unfamiliar with the temporary Cedula card, and what it signified. In the end, a supervisor was called and Paul, my friend, was granted re-admittance.

FROM THE STREET

I was a member of the ARCR and cannot say that I was 100% satisfied. They responded to one of my questions over email within a few days. However, after I sent a second question, I have waited months and resubmitted the question 3 different times. I even wrote to the general email address to complain that the legal department had not returned my email. They wrote back stating the system is having glitches. I still haven't received an answer to my immigration question.

Paul Ford is an expat living his *pura vida* in the Central Pacific Coast. He saved a ton of time and coin by securing all of the needed documents with the appropriate notary and government seals before arriving to Costa Rica. He then used ARCR to facilitate his application process. He reported that he was pleased with their response time to his questions and with the overall experience. About 6 months and $1200 later, he held his cedula in his hand.

Sandra Brooks tackled with residency for almost 7 years! She said looking back, *"Don't go to an attorney unless they specialize in residency and even then get a referral."* She arrived in Costa Rica with her husband in 2004. They qualified for residency and placed a large sum of money in a Costa Rican bank.

Their lawyer insisted that the money had to stay in the bank over the five years they worked with him. (Of course that is not true. The money just needs to pass through a Costa Rican bank, get converted to Colones, and then you can do with it what you wish). They spent over $3,000 on an incompetent attorney. After many wrong roads, Sandra finally landed at Residency in Costa Rica with Javier Zavelata (www.ResidencyinCostaRica.com). Javier and his sister Maria are Ticos who run their business from the US. Maria is in the US embassy daily, so much so, the guards even open the door for her when they see her coming. Sandra reports that these two Ticos know how to get it done! She didn't wait in one line nor return to the States. They did everything for her, even her police report!

Congratulations! You have either figured out how you can legally ascertain your cedula or have decided on the path more traveled, the perpetual tourist! Now, where to land?

PART II

IT'S PERSONAL

FIND WHERE IN COSTA RICA IS RIGHT FOR YOU, CUSTOMIZED COST OF
LIVING, AND A BREAKDOWN OF TRANSPORTATION OPTIONS

WHERE IN COSTA RICA IS YOUR PARADISE?

FINDING YOUR SLICE OF HEAVEN IS ALL ABOUT WASPS

Deciding what you want in your dream home can be daunting, not to worry! I, along with many other expats, have paved the way and can help you avoid the mistakes that we have made.

Where you decide to land in Costa Rica could make or break your experience. Think back to the vacations and towns you've loved the most. There is an energy inside of you that comes alive in the right environment, where you glow and happiness is less elusive. You may already know that when you're in the mountains that part of you is electrified, or maybe it's the beach or downtown metropolis that tickles you.

Regardless, the surefire way to choose your slice of heaven is to consider the big picture: W.A.S.P.S.- Weather, Activity/Amenities, Setting, Proximity to airport, and Social requirements.

WEATHER

As mentioned in the **Basics** section, Costa Rica has a variety of excellent climate options. You need to know what you prefer. If you are looking for sunny and 70, don't go to the coast. The central valley is your bread and butter! If you want hot and sweaty then the coast is your domain. Do you enjoy fall weather? Make sure you know the answer to that question before you look at regions because it will save you valuable time and money.

To see detailed weather reports of each region in Costa Rica visit:

http://www.guaduabamboo.com/costa-rica-climate.html

ACTIVITIES

What *activities* do you want access to on a regular basis? Do you want to live near hiking trails, hot springs, caves, expansive beaches, volcanos, waterfalls, streams or bustling metropolis with an active nightlife and entertainment options? Do you plan to keep your mind active with hobbies, part time work, volunteering in your community, or social endeavors?

A life lounging by the pool becomes devoid of purpose after the initial high wears off and your batteries recharged. For young adults without kids looking for a hip place to meet people like yourselves, don't buy a house in an isolated jungle on the Osa Peninsula! You will be bored and your social requirements will not be satisfied. If you seek *night life* and *social events,* make sure your location can deliver. If your idea of perfection is a relaxing path less traveled, don't opt for hot spots like Jaco and Montezuma.

AMENITIES

No two places are created equal and each place has it's trade offs. What *amenities* are "must haves"? Do you want to be isolated, in an urban area, suburb, or somewhere in between? When you reach lush jungles in your apartment/house search, you may not have other utilities. Think about and decide "What are your deal breakers?" Do you require cable internet or would a 3g stick[6] work for you? Do you need to live in a place where electricity rarely fails and where the water supply is consistent? Or are you a candle toting adventurer willing to get away from it all, including electricity from time to time to delve deeper into untouched beauty?

SETTING

Are you a birder? Do you want to live in an area that is known for it's excellent birding like Monteverde? Or maybe you would prefer to enjoy your daily walk in the jungle and spot an Ocelot or a family of monkeys. Do you dream of views of the ocean wrapped with jungle, or volcanos, rivers, or waterfalls? Do you want to be around a large or small community or are you looking for isolation?

PROXIMITY TO AIRPORT

Do you wish to reside close to the airport or is it exciting to live down a 3 hour dirt road? How far away is too far? Be advised, Google Maps may work for directions but fails miserable at time estimation. Talk to a local or look at a bus schedule for best estimates.

Along with *proximity to the airport* you have to decide what *setting* your dream house is located in? Do you imagine yourself amongst the clouds in the cloud forest, along an expansive coconut palmed lined beach, near mangroves that you can kayak through, deep in the forest or jungle near pumas, in a birder's heaven, near a lake or on one of the

---

[6] A 3G stick is a USB device that provides a much slower and less reliable internet connection based on a cellular plan to which you subscribe

hundreds of rivers that you can fly-fish, kayak or white-water raft down? Make sure to research that your area satisfies these desires.

SOCIAL REQUIREMENTS

Whether you're single or married, you need to decide what types of social interaction you wish to have close by. A lush getaway in the jungle may be romantic in it's ideal but if you are an extravert and you have no neighbors, with this would not be a great option for you.

MOUNTAINS VS. BEACH

Are you a mountain goat or a beach bum? If you were raised in the mountains, there is a good chance that you will feel more at home in the crisp air surrounded by mountains, volcanos, and waterfalls. If you were raised on the coast, the ebb and flow of the water will be your lullaby.

Ok, so what if you're not from either or have lived in both or just plan don't know! If you are sensitive to the tropical and sometimes oppressive heat, something in the mountains or valleys would suit you better. The Central Valley boasts 72 degrees Fahrenheit year round with minimal rain fall. The Valley hosts numerous active and inactive volcanos, lakes, rivers, and offers quick access to the largest international airport in Costa Rica, Juan Santamaría International Airport (SJO) and every market imaginable in San Jose.

As an added bonus, the cost of living is noticeably cheaper inland. The difference is most noticeable on property/rent and the cost of local produce! Fuel prices are regulated across the country so don't worry about finding the cheapest place to fill up, instead focus on the service or proximity to your residence.

TO SUM UP

Now that you have a grasp on *WHAT* you want, lets walk through *WHERE* in Costa Rica offers your perfect combination of wants and needs.

Costa Rica has seven provinces / regions: *Guanacaste, Alajuela, Heredia, Limón, Cartago, San José, & Puntarenas.* They are structured much like the States.

GUANACASTE

- Population: 326,953
- Driest & warmest providence
- Liberia International Airport
- Host to numerous resorts in the northwest region
- Cowboy country

Guanacaste has it all: valleys, volcanos, cowboys, packed surfer towns, and sun! Because it's the driest and warmest providence in CR, make sure that you hydrate and take advantage of the readily available pipa fría *(cold coconut water)*.

With it's heavy cowboy presence, you could call it the "wild west" of CR. In addition to cowboys, the region is known for birdwatching, rodeos, surfing, and dry tropical forests.

The dirt roads with the exception of the costañera, are all considered "back roads" and are pot-hole ridden. Driving during the dry season produces a relentless dust-cloud. Pedestrians along the road are often seen armed with handkerchiefs around their mouths in an attempt to decrease the amount of dirt they inhale.

While Guanacaste is the most sparsely populated region in the country, it is home to some pretty big surf spots. As the largest surfing hub in Guanacaste, **Tamarindo** packs them in. There, beginners and pros alike rub elbows in gorgeous blue bath-temperature water. After a surf lesson, there are plenty of expats wandering about to befriend and share a beer with.

Travel just 20 minutes to the north and arrive at **Brasilito**, a pueblo less traveled with respectively less amenities. What it lacks in amenities, it makes up for with a rich authentic Tico charm. It is here that you can escape from the "crazy" while remaining only 20 minutes away from large grocery stores, a plethora of social interactions, and doctors offices.

Cañas, home to the Centro de Rescate Las Pumas *(Puma Rescue Center),* is located in the low lands which means it will be hot! It is a central gateway to Lake Arenal and Palo Verde National Park.

Guanacaste also hosts the oldest city in Costa Rica. **Nicoya** was alive and well inhabited by Chorotega Indians before the arrival of the Spaniards.

EXPERIENCE

My boyfriend and I were headed up the mountain towards Monteverde from Papagayo. The sun had just set and it got dark fast! Jason and I were exhausted, a storm was rolling in, and the roads were very difficult to navigate at night so we thought it best to find a hotel. We saw a sign for a hotel /resort and followed it onto questionable roads. At one time, our car's left front and right rear wheels were off the ground the road was tweaked so badly. The car teetered and started sliding back. It didn't take long before our tiny 2-wheel drive rental car got stuck in the clay. We were stranded, hungry and tired. In fact, we had found the hotel in question but since it was boarded up and deserted, I thought that couldn't have been it and pressed onward. I was deeply regretting that decision. I called the Red Cross and they said they would help but never returned my call so I set out to find a Tico to see if they could help us. Coincidentally, after a 20 minute walk down the mountain, I found the nephew of the owner of the hotel that we had detoured for. The boy ran and got his uncle who loaded up 7 Ticos and me into his truck. We bumped down the mountain towards our car. It was at this time that the skies opened up in a fury. The owner hooked up our car to his with a tow hook and managed to get us down the winding hill. At one point our car was close to flipping over and going over the edge of the mountain. He ran out of gas half way through towing us but simply ran home and got some more fuel, then returned to finish his good deed. The Ticos were all laughing in the rain, as we were a great sense of entertainment to them with our tired grumpiness. The owner told us he had shut down his hotel some time ago. It wasn't funny then, but I can't help but laugh now thinking back to the fact that the the owner ended up rescuing us from the situation that he inadvertently caused.
~ *Chris, Florida*

W   A   S   P   S

Weather

🌞SUNNY

🌞87-96 degree F *(31-36 C)* highs year round, with lows averaging 69-89 degrees F *(21-32 C)*

🌞Rainfall: varies greatly depending on which part of Guanacaste and which season. As low as 0'' during the dry season and as much as 127.9'' in one month during the wet season! Morning rain is rare, afternoon and night showers occur frequently during the wet season.

Humidity: 61%-87% year round

Activities/Amenities

Guanacaste's larger towns like Tamarindo and Nicoya offer every amenity that one desires within walking distance including medical offices. It also offers consistent cable, water, and electricity *(as consistent as Costa Rica gets that is)*.

Activities vary depending on what part of Guanacaste you reside in but can include:

- Sea kayaking
- Windsurfing / Kitesurfing
- Beach bunny/ surfing
- Scuba diving / snorkeling
- Boating/ fishing
- Shopping
- Horseback riding
- Mountain trekking
- Birding
- Cultural activities
- Hiking
- Volcano Exploration
- Visit National Parks and Reserves

Housing options also vary city to pueblo. Apartments, condos, high rises, townhouses, self sustained communities, and farms are all available in the region. Internet will vary depending on location. The larger towns such as Tamarindo will have cable, but some of the towns set up in the hills will only connect via a 3g stick.

Setting Options

- Cloud forest
- Volcanos
- Dry forest
- Beach
- Riverside
- Basin/ flatland

Proximity to Airport

1 hour from the Daniel Oduber International Airport in Liberia which will run at least $70 USD by taxi and $3 USD by bus. It's a 5 hour drive from the larger SJO in Alajuela by shuttle van, ($50 USD). A bus will run you $10 USD.

Social Offerings

In towns like Tamarindo, Flamingo, Papagayo, Playas del Coco, or Nicoya, there are plenty of locals, tourists, and expats with which to mingle. They are more timeshare / resort destinations so you will feel that vibe as well. If you are looking for isolation, take to the mountains or small pueblos between larger beach towns. T

If you are weary of crowds, Tamarindo is not the location for you. Hundreds and sometimes thousands of tourists flood the beaches during high season. It is a backpackers' haven. If you're looking for a strong surfer expat community, you will find it in Tamarindo. For more isolation and peace and quiet, take it to Bahía de Los Pirates, Playa Minas, or Puerto Viejo *(Pacific Side)*.

ALAJUELA

Population: 848,146
SJO airport
Poás Volcano
Arenal Volcano
Mild temperatures

Being raised in San Diego, people around the country ask me "What it was like to have it sunny and 70 all year round?" To tell you the truth, that is not an accurate portrayal of San Diego, but it does describe the central valley of the Alajuela Providence.

Besides phenomenal weather, Alajuela is known for it's active volcanos Arenal and Poás plus it's five national parks. As a providence filled with forests, mountains, volcanoes, and rivers, Alajuela is where Costa Rican history collides with nature.

San Ramón, Sarchí, and Zarcero are three culturally rich options for residence.

San Ramón

is known for hosting presidents and poets alike. With roughly 70,000 residents, San Ramón is no pueblo. The city blends the unique Costa

Rican flavor with widely available and affordable medical and dental care, american style shopping, restaurants, and the hustle and bustle that comes with city living. If you are looking to move your US city life to CR for better cost of living, this city might be your best option. It provides bowling, US brand stores, English flicks, and world class medical facilities.

There is an excellent expat community in San Ramón where many have chosen to put their hands to good use through a volunteer program called The Community Action Alliance. The alliance is a blend of expats and Ticos determined to make a difference. Gringos and Ticos together have raised money for retirement homes, orphanages, and animal rescue centers. http://actionalliancecr.com

The University of Costa Rica is located in San Ramón which means you will have cultural events, concerts, and art galleries available to you!

Most expats in this area find homes in the hills and mountains surrounding the town in semi-rural settings which average 35 minutes to an hour away from the main airport, SJO.

Sarchí

is located just 30 Km northwest of the SJO airport. This is the country's most famous artisan town, a true hub for artistic and cultural expression. The region is best known for it's hand painted ox carts.[7]

Sarchí is a great base hub for visiting neighboring Poás and Barva volcanos. It's also just minutes for the automotive hub of the country, Grecia. Everyone and anyone will tell you that the best deal on a car or car parts is in Grecia. The shift from urban to artisan can easily be observed the second you enter Grecia. Souvenirs, furniture stores, and elegant woodwork quickly infiltrate each side of the street. Even if

---

[7] For more on ox carts see **Basics**

Sarchí isn't your slice of heaven, it's an excellent place to order custom woodwork or pick up home furnishings.

Zarcero

Elevation of 1,736 meters (5,696 feet)

Have you ever driven through a town and decided you absolutely have to try out living in that magical place? This happened tome. I was on a road trip in Costa Rica with a friend and we were incessantly lamenting about the beauty and magic of this hillside community. We were so enthralled that I "dropped a pin" in my iPhone map and labeled it, "Must live here!" Approximately 400 feet later Ginger, my 1980 CJ7 Jeep, broke down. Ginger lent fate a helping hand. I could not get her into gear. Each attempt felt empty, then I heard a large *whack*. I cringed as I heard the loud sound of something important falling off of my car and onto the ground. I bent down and saw the drive shaft lying on the asphalt. Dang, that looks important, I thought. Ok... No problem, I just have to find a mechanic and show him this chunk of metal and he will probably find the answer to my little problem.

A friendly Tico walked by and I asked him where could I find the nearest mechanic. He pointed to a house at the bottom of the hill. I found my *Tico angel*[8] in a local mechanic who let us sit in his home while he figured out how to repair Ginger. We had to stay in **Zarcero** overnight while he waited on a part from a neighboring town.

He called a cab to take us to nearby hotel, where we fell in love with Zarcero. The town's courtyard lined with manicured hedges in numerous shapes and archways enchanted us. We savored the autumn-like brisk air that the locals promise last all year long. I fell in love with the

---

Clockwise from top left: Papagayo, Papagayo, Paquera, Playa Conchal, Papagayo
[8] Tico Angel is a term used by many expats to explain the common phenomenon where a gringo is in a bind and a caring Tico comes to their rescue.

charming locals. They were so happy, charismatic, and hospitable. We also enjoyed the fact that the only gringos we saw were each other!

A short drive out of town leads you to cloud forests encased in fog and majesty. While this was gorgeous, it did make driving a bit difficult and dangerous. After you descend out of the clouds, about 45 minutes of driving will grant you arrival at the SJO airport!

W   A   S   P   S

Weather

If you are looking for the perfect 72 degree weather with sun on most days, this is the region for you. It varies slightly depending on your altitude since there are a variety of mountains and volcanos in the region.

Activities/Amenities

There are a variety of excellent hiking opportunities in the region due to its two active volcanos, Poás and Arenal. There are also ample hot springs. In the past, you could see hot lava flowing out of Arenal's crater but the flow stopped in 2010. The giant is active but sleeping. Other activities in the area include:

- Kayaking in Lake Arenal
- Visiting one of the 5 national parks and numerous wild refuges
- Boating/ fishing
- Cultural events
- Shopping
- Horseback riding
- Mountain trekking

- Birding
- Hiking
- White water rafting / kayaking

There are a variety of housing options in Alajuela ranging from high-end custom homes built inside eco-societies amongst the mountains to modest Tico style rentals inside or outside of major towns.

Setting Options

City living, valley living, riverside, lakeside, or a hide-away in the mountains are all possible in this region. Each setting has pluses and minuses. The further up the mountains you venture, the further away you are from the services offered by the city.

Proximity to Airport

You are in luck! The Alajuela region includes the city Alajuela where the larger of the two international airports resides! SJO is located in the southern portion of the providence. In case becoming a perpetual tourist is your means of immigration, the providence also borders Nicaragua to the north making those border jumps all the more accessible.

Social Offerings

As the second largest populated region in CR, there are plenty of opportunities for social interaction. Language skills would greatly enhance social interaction. While there are expat pockets in places like La Fortuna, San Carlos, and San Ramón, Spanish skills would greatly advance your social opportunities and overall experience. As mentioned above, San Ramón has an excellent established community-lead program called *The Community Action Alliance* where you can get connected and make a difference alongside Ticos!

HEREDIA

- Population: 433,677
- Barva Volcano
- Braulio Carrillo National Park
- Tapantí National Park
- La Selva - Birders Mecca

The city of Heredia is the second largest in Costa Rica, hosting numerous jobs and major Universities for Ticos. The region expands north to the Nicaraguan border where the land is agriculturally rich. Host to the Sarapiqui River, it is known as a white water and kayaking destination.

One prominent neotropical study sites, La Selva Biological Station is not only important to the advancement of science, it is also a birder's Mecca. If birding is your passion, take advantage of their day or overnight stays! Contact the office of the Organization for Tropical Studies for overnight stays at +506-240-6696, contact the station at +506-766-6565 for day visits.

When Coffee was introduced to CR, the fertile volcanic soil offered by Barva became one of many ideal crop locations.

Heredia

Heredia is also known as the city of flowers. There are three possible reasons for this. The first provides the most common explanation told to tourists which is because most of the exotic flowers that CR exports are produced in the city of Heredia. The second reason for the nickname could be to represent the gorgeous woman in Heredia. Some say they are second to none in the country. The third possibility, and mentioned the least, is the wealthy Flores family who used their resources to pressure political and social initiatives. They have been described as a Costa Rican mob family.

While the Flores family greatly impacted politics of the 19th Century, they had no control over the churches. Heredia is home to the oldest church in CR dating back to 1797! Early Costa Rican construction centered each town around the church so the community had a place to meet and a way to stay connected. While this tradition is still alive and well in the overwhelmingly Catholic nation, soccer fields have popped up in each town offering a new modern and secular way to interact.

In addition to soccer fields, the country's largest University, the National University of Costa Rica located in the city of Heredia, offers another way for Ticos to connect. The college also accepts many international students! Heredia is an excellent place to live if you are planning to teach English. There are a plethora of English academies and private tutoring opportunities.

San Isidro

The gateway city for all of the surrounding agricultural communities and for famed Chirripó National Park is San Isidro. Fruit plantations, flower farms, and especially delicious pineapples line the Talamanca mountains.

Besides fruit, you have excellent odds of spotting the resplendent quetzal bird. One of the most valued and admired birds in Central America, it thrives in the San Isidro area. Visit nearby Reserva de Aves Neotropicales Los Cusingos for more excellent birding in the 350 acre *(142 hectares)* zone!

The region is arguably the fastest growing region in Costa Rica. San Isidro is the gateway to the gorgeous southern beaches of Dominical, Uvita, and Playa Ojochal *(1-1.5 hr drive)*, along with access to the central valley.

Big exports in the region include sugar cane, pineapple, and coffee. San Isidro is host to the largest farmers co-op in the country.

Don't be mistaken, the city itself is quite urban with numerous amenities including: modern medical and dental clinics, full service hospital, insurance, legal services, libraries, movie theaters, banks, parks, Spanish language schools, and two universities.

Sarapiquí

Traversing from the Caribbean Sea to the northern slopes of the Barva and Poás Volcanos the river Sarapiqui ranges from tranquil to vengeful. The río hosts more whitewater thrill-seekers than any other body of water in CR. The further upstream the river, the more rage fills the waters. North of San Miguel is downright suicidal! From San Miguel to La Virgen, class IV-V rapids meet you at every turn.

In-between the white knuckle rapids, make sure and appreciate the two and three-fingered sloths dangling above in the trees and the howler monkeys cheering you on. River otters, crocodiles, and a variety of birds are all visible along the way.

W A S P S

Weather

Heredia is a long narrow province that offers a variety of climates. There are the warm humid lowlands south of Nicaragua, cool and wet highlands in the mountains, and of course, the mild climate of the Central Valley.

Activities/Amenities

- Excellent birding!
- Hiking- including a volcano climb
- Whitewater rafting / kayaking
- Camping
- Trekking
- Fishing/ Fly fishing
- National Park and Wildlife Refuges
- Hospital
- Movie Theaters
- Banks

Setting Options

Heredia province, like many of the provinces, offers a range of settings including: urban, agricultural, mountain, riverside, volcanic, and lowland hot tropics.

Proximity to Airport

Depending on where in the province you choose to live, the drive time to SJO airport will range from 30 minutes to 3.5 hours.

Social Offerings

Heredia offers the spectrum of social opportunities from college life in the heart of urban Heredia city, to isolated mountain or jungle living. In between the social extremes exist pockets of Tico towns like Sarapiquí. With a 22% growth rate, San Isidro is also rapidly becoming an expat hub. Expect to hear more from this region.

LIMÓN

- Population: 386,862
- Caribbean lowlands
- Most culturally diverse
- Reggae
- Rain throughout the year

Bob Marley meets surf-hobo with a sprinkling of tropical bliss describes much of the Caribbean coast of Costa Rica. While Limón as a province offers less diversity regarding climate and setting options, it is the most ethnically diverse region in CR.

Caribbean Costa Rica does not follow the same season rules as the rest of the country. There is no "dry" season, instead rain is consistent throughout the year with pockets of dry weeks. This leaves the shores a lush green. This wetland also brings with it a slight chance of malaria. Check the CDC website for current warnings and consult your physician if you are concerned. The occurrence is extremely low, 48 per 100,000 last measured. I am personally comfortable with the application of repellent to my clothes and exposed skin while traversing the wettest region in the nation, Tortuguero National Park. This region is home to the highest occurrence of malaria. Southern *Carib* has not had a large outbreak of malaria in the last 5 years and only one outbreak of Dengue Fever half a decade ago.

Limón is an urban port city through and through. In case you haven't been to a port town, it's dirty, criminally active, and overall unpleasant. It is a place to catch a ride out. Be extra mindful of your belongings and suspicious people while in the city.

The United Fruit Company paved the way for the main source of income in the region. This success, ironically, was a direct result of a failure.

It took the government over 15 years to complete the railway from San José to Limón. Malaria, heat stroke, and malnutrition killed much of the work force. In order to save money, the American businessman in-charge of the railroad project, Minor Keith, placed banana plants along the tracks being constructed to serve as food for the workers.

Once completed, the railways were unsuccessful attracting passengers. Frustrated, Keith ordered every empty passenger car to be filled with bananas to ship to the United States. Thus the creation of the United Fruit Company.

Limón can thank the railroads for being the most culturally diverse region in CR. The railroad construction brought in thousands of Jamaicans, Chinese, and Italian laborers. In addition to a cultural melting pot, this means the food is awesome and options are vast! The railroad service closed in 1991.

The Costa Rica Railway Institute is currently revamping the railroads. The Institute has been slowly bringing routes back since 2005. Most available routes are in and around San José.

⦿2005: Pavas - San José
⦿2009: Heredia - San José
⦿2011: San Antonio de Belén - San José
⦿2013: Cartago - San José

The goal is to relieve some of the atrocious congestion in San José during rush hour. The cost is rarely over a dollar and is about equivalent to bus fare. For the train schedule and routes see:

http://www.horariodetren.com/EN/cr/

Puerto Viejo de la Talmanca

This town takes Rastafari to the next level. If the smell and sight of Mary Jane[9] makes you uncomfortable, this is not the town for you. The last time I visited this sleepy surf town, a waitress had to put down her lit homemade joint in order to ring me up. I'm pretty sure they sell more Bob Marley paraphernalia than Costa Rican souvenirs.

Besides peace and love, Puerto Viejo is home to an idyllic Caribbean coast where coral reefs checker the coastline like a beautiful puzzle easily seen through the transparent warm caribbean water.

Tortuguero

Tortuguero literally translates to home of the turtles. The great endangered leatherback turtles, green sea turtles, hawksbills, and loggerheads have been flocking there for years to lay thousands of eggs. Which is precisely why the government decided to protect the area dubbing it a National Park.

Despite the difficult access, it is the 3rd most visited park in Costa Rica. You can only reach the region by plane or boat. The water-level in the area is in constant flux. Because rivers, mangroves, estuaries, and

---

[9] Marijuana, reefer, hash

the ocean surround the little village, the "docks" are more a verbal ideal than actual location. In actuality, the dock is wherever the waterline meets a tree where the captain can tie his boat.

In addition to being a National Park, Tortuguero is not a city or town, it's a village. There is no ATM or bank, only a few restaurants and hotels so plan accordingly.

My last visit ended early due to flooding. Because the village is surrounded by water in each direction, after a torrential downpour, it can take days for the water to recede. While trekking through knee deep water, I overhead a local say in Spanish, "This is worse than when we evacuated all of the gringos a few years back." That was my cue to exit. To read more about my Tortuguero adventure, see the following *Experience* section.

If off the grid is what you desire, Tortuguero is a moist nature saturated option.

In order to get back on the grid, there is 2 hour boat ride from Tortuguero to Limón through a canal that parallels the Caribbean Sea. I saw more animals on this ride than I did on any animal seeking tourism tour. I was entertained by sloths, monkeys, pink flamingos, blue heron, toucans, caiman, and a variety of other birds.

After you arrive to Limón, there will be taxi vans waiting to pick you up for the 20 min ride to Puerto Viejo de la Talmanca for about $10 USD. The cheaper option is to walk about a quarter mile to the bus station and catch a bus to PV, Cahuita or onward to Manzanilla.

EXPERIENCE

During my trip to Tortuguero I learned that Ticos use "dock" very loosely. First off, there were no wood or cement structures to tie up a vessel. Instead, there were trees along a shoreline and small six to seven foot boats tied up to keep them "secured." The locals explained that the location of these "docks" could be hundreds of feet away depending on the amount of rainfall they had recently. The international travelers and locals alike disembarked from our antique bus and climbed aboard our trusty dingy with our confident captain that proclaimed we could indeed all fit without sinking. I couldn't help but notice there were only a few life vests on the boat, but after all, we were in Costa Rica. "Relax", I told myself. It took about 30 seconds after we pushed off from our tree to encounter our first major problem.

It seemed the steering wheel was not working. Somehow the connection between the one outboard motor and the steering column had become disconnected. Meanwhile, the front of the boat was drifting into a section of barbed wire (why there was barbed wire in the middle of swamp land I have yet to figure out). Our captain's trusty deckhand was on the bow of the boat and noticed the wire just in time to jump over it and grab hold of a sand bar. Once temporarily secured to the sand bar, I looked over to where we had almost drifted. Only to see a raging river charging the opposite direction of travel, churning with a vengeance. "Ok," I said to myself, "Now it's time to worry." I have whitewater experience and know that if we would have drifted into this raging river at our current angle, we would have been flipped like a burger at McDonalds! The captain apparently noticed because he rolled open the plastic windows (which were previously blocking the rain, and would have also blocked our emergency exit in the event of a rollover).

The captain also proceeded to place the few life jackets available onto the children in the vessel. So I recapped to myself, even the captain thinks we are going to flip. He proceeded to talk to the passengers in Spanish, "I was really wishing I had studied more Spanish right about now." Just when I thought I could not be any more terrified I remembered that there were caiman and alligators in these waters... Then, our leader devised a plan. He commanded his deckhand to hold the throttles, freeing him to climb to the back of the small boat and direct the outboard by manually pushing it right or left as needed. When he needed more or less speed he simply shouted to his compadre. The moment of truth came when we shoved off the sand bar and held our breath as we entered the furious water. The captain skillfully commanded the appropriate entry speeds and angles to keep the vessel upright. Thirty minutes of whitewater and white knuckles later, we entered a large thruway, allowing the rest of our two and a half hour journey a more copacetic ride.

Cahuita

Cahuita is a town within biking distance north of Puerto Viejo de la Talmanca. With only 4,000 residents, it offers a sleepy feel of afro-caribbean influence. You are likely to hear more Creole or Patois than Spanish.

Choose between black or white sand beaches inside Cahuita National Park. The coral reef offshore is one of the best preserved marine filled reefs in the nation.

Manzanilla

Take the chill vibe in Puerto Viejo and take it down yet another notch and you have Manzanilla. Less activity, less entertainment, and more exotic empty beaches. Manzanilla is romantic, relaxing, and gorgeous with the enormous blue morpho butterflies fluttering everywhere.

There are only a few hotels and restaurants in the area. Zero local municipalities leave nearby PV as your access to city utilities like I.C.E. *(electric and phone company)* and larger grocery stores.

W   A   S   P   S

Weather

The southern Caribbean Coast is sunny with frequent storms. The average temperature is around 84 degrees with little variance. The black sand beaches absorb the hot sun and create a heavy blanket of heat that hovers over the beach. It can feel like walking across black asphalt on a hot day.

Activities/Amenities

- Scuba diving/ snorkeling
- Kayaking
- Surfing
- Learn Creole
- Afro-Carib food
- Sloth rescue
- Sea turtle viewing
- Beach walks
- Fishing/ Boating

Setting Options

There are fewer mountain options in the Limón province. Most established communities reside along the Caribbean Coast creating a wide range of beachside living. In many areas on the Caribbean, the jungle collides with the sea giving you an opportunity to have both atmospheres at your front porch.

Proximity to Airport

SJO is your closest airport ranging from 3-5 hours away depending on where you settle.

Social Offerings

Areas such as Manzanilla don't have large populations let alone communities of expats, but as PV overfills, Manzanilla is picking up a few people here and there. I expect this town to slowly fill in. Puerto Viejo De La Talmanca is the Caribbean hub for expats, an international melting pot. Restaurant reggae concerts, surf contests, and social events will be an every weekend occurrence here soon.

CARTAGO

Population: 490,903

Rich colonial tradition

La Negrita

Basílica de Nuestra Señora de Los Ángeles

Costa Rica Institute of Technology

Río Reventazón

This province is known for its rich ecological diversity, dense tropical rain forests, rich colonial traditions, Black Madonna, and the whitewater thrill ride courtesy of Río Reventazón.

Driving through and around the mountains shock the surveyor with vibrant green and exotic flora and fauna. You are certain with each bend that *it* is the prettiest section of Costa Rica you have ever seen, until the next turn when, in fact, *that* must be the most gorgeous site you have ever seen!

The province is tucked in by Volcán Irazú and Turrialba to the north, and Cerro de la Muerte and Mount Chirripó to the south. The five national parks, two volcanos, two major rivers and many mountains translate to an endless supply of breathtaking scenery, outdoor activities, and nature to be explored.

Nearly 50% of the bird species found in Cerro de la Muerto are endemic, meaning they are only found in Costa Rica and western Panama. Examples include: Fiery-throated hummingbird, Timberline Wren, Black-Billed Nightingale-Thrush, Sooty Robin, and Volcano Junco.

Río Reventazón is visited by more whitewater enthusiasts than any other river in CR. The most common section traveled is a Class III stretch from Tucurrique to Turrialba. Venturing on either side of this section is more dangerous and technical skills are required.

After the government run power company, I.C.E., placed a damn, one third of the class IV rapids along the Reventazón have dwindled. This was the first of four dams to be placed for hydroelectricity production. The project is intended to deal with increased demands. According to the World Bank, energy consumption per capita has increased 73% since 1975.

Residents of Turrialba held a plebiscite, or vote, regarding the damns and because a staggering 97% of the residents proclaimed a resounding "no" the project was shelved until 2016.

Irazú Volcano National Park

Irazú gets its name from an indian word, istarú, which translates to "mountain of thunder." Something that you remember if you have any sense of self preservation while climbing towards the cone of this powerful beast.

Hiking the volcano can prove quite a feat. The summit is above the tree line at 11,260 feet (3,432m) so shade is not a commodity often found. The volcano reaches higher in the sky than any other in Costa Rica. The impact from the past eruptions of Irazú is in evidence the higher you trek with less and less vegetation and the sight of scorched dead tree trunks. Birders can spot the Volcán Junco and Volcano Hummingbird here.

The last series of eruptions was between August of 1962 and March of 1965.

The volcano has twin craters. The smaller of the two, Diego de la Haya Crater, has a mineral rich lake that changes hues from emerald green to blood red.

The park is open from 8:00am- 3:30pm but cloud-cover often thickens by 10am so try to arrive early. Park admission is $10 USD per person and parking is $2.20 USD.

Tapantí-Macizo la Muerte National Park

Known simply as Tapantí, it was declared a National Park in 1982. A higher elevation rain forest at 3,950 - 8,350ft *(1,200 - 2,550m)* allows the park to host a diverse collection of flora and fauna. Bring your rain coat to explore the unique offerings of Tapantí because the park sees rain almost daily. In addition to rain the park sees anteaters, jaguars, monkeys, tapirs, and river otters. There are over 260 different bird species to view.

For hikers, well marked trails zig-zag throughout the park. Don't miss the easy hike to Sendero La Catarata boasting a picture perfect waterfall to reward your stroll.

There is also fishing in the park. The river is stocked with rainbow trout, and with a valid fishing license, you are permitted to pluck five fish per day from the río between April 1st and October 31st as long as they are over 25 centimeters. The park is open from 8:00am-4:00pm. Admission is $10 USD.

Braulio Carrillo National Park

The drive through the park is absolutely breath-taking. Even without leaving the car, you can see this was a special forest destined for adoration and needing protection.

With elevations ranging from 118 feet (36 m) to 9,500 feet (2,900 m) Braulio has it all! You can trek through the rain forest, along the streams and rivers, or amongst the clouds in the cloud forest.

Explore the uncrowded yet well maintained trails to waterfalls and overlooks. There are over 32 miles of trails inside the park. Start your walk in the high elevation rain forest and end it with a bonfire at the beach in Cahuita!

While adventuring, don't forget to stow your rain jacket. Expect to use it each afternoon you spend in the park.

The park is open from 8:00am-4:00pm and will run you $7 USD.

Chirripó National Park

Chirripó National Park is one of the wilder parks and home to Costa Rica's highest peak, Cerro Chirripó. If you can manage the difficult 11 mile (18km) scramble to the top, on a clear day you are rewarded with views of both the Pacific Ocean and the Caribbean Sea simultaneously! This is no easy 11 mile hike. The elevation gain is nearly 10,000 feet (3,000m)!

There is a hut equipped with bunk bed sleeping racks near the peak where you can crash overnight if you don't want to make the roundtrip hike in one shot. You will tromp through more ecological zones in this one park than you will find in most countries. Stop by the ranger station and ask for a permit before attempting the climb.

While you are near the ranger station, walk north for about 15 minutes and arrive in San Gerardo de Rivas. Look for the hand painted sign that guides you to the right. The hot spring pool is on private property, so if the owner or his kids ask you for a buck to use the pool, fork it over. It is well worth the view and the soothing of your achy muscles.

The park is a popular Tico destination, so unless you want to trek in a line with other adventurers avoid it during the weekends in the dry season and the week of Semana Santa *(Easter break)*.

Turrialba Volcano National Park

Measuring in at 10,950 ft (3,340m), Turrialba is no volcano to be overlooked, but often is. After almost a century of sleeping, the seldom visited giant woke up in January of 2010 and remains active to this day. More recently in 2012, scientists noted sulfuric gas and ash escaping from a new vent. The groggy volcano is named after the Huetar Indian words turiri and abá which collectively mean "river of fire."

A dirt road will take you close to the top, whereafter you can proceed by foot through a steep zig-zag trail. The switchbacks, however, are not for the faint of heart. You must be in reasonably good shape to attempt the brutal climb. There are no facilities within the park. Plan ahead with plenty of food, water, sun protection, and layers to wear.

If the summit is open, the risk-takers have a chance to peer into the center crater and observe minor fumarole activity in the bubbling sulfur-rich mud.

Cartago

The air is cooler in Cartago with an elevation of 4,707 feet (1,435m). The town itself serves as a commercial and residential center. However, a short drive around the bend leads you to mountains that will shock and delight you with their vibrance of life. Cartago is a resilient town surviving three major earthquakes and the rage of Volcán Irazú in 1963.

Cartago was the first capital of Costa Rica until 1823. The town is best known for La Negrita, a mulatta (mixed race) patron saint commonly referred to as the Black Madonna. The statue is known for having great healing powers. The folktale is that the statue was found by an indigenous girl in 1635. She brought it home but shortly thereafter, it mysteriously disappeared. She later found the statue in it's original location. She repeatedly brought it home only to have it disappear later to reappear in it's original site.

Another site of spiritual importance is Basílica de Nuestra Señora de Los Ángeles *(Basilica of Our Lady of the Angels)*. There is a pilgrimage consisting of thousands of people to this location every year on August 2nd for the feast day of the Virgin of the Angels.

Turrialba

A small bustling town just 40 miles (65 Kilometers) from San José and at 2130 ft (650m) elevation, Turrialba exudes an authentic Tico-agricultural feel with sugar cane, coffee farms, and dense forest wrapping the town like a blanket. There are not many expats here yet, but as thousands of gringos are "imported" each year, I believe it's just a matter of time before this gem is revealed from it's case.

The occasional gringos seen walking around town are usually in route to test their skills in Rió Reventazón or Río Pacuare.

Orosí

Orosí is a small village known for its coffee farms, its Lago de Cachí (hot springs), and its beautifully preserved Iglesia de San José de Orosí, the oldest functioning church in Costa Rica (built from 1743-66).

W A S P S

Weather

- 75-78 F (24-25 C) highs
- 51-58 F (10-15 C) lows
- Cooler in the mountains, especially Cerro de la Muerte

Surrounded by two volcanos and two mountains, the Reventazón River Valley is protected by moisture brought in by the winds making it the second driest province in the country *(second to Guanacaste)*. The higher elevation allows for more clouds and pleasant temperatures year round.

Activities/Amenities

- Irazú Volcano National Park
- Tapantí National Park
- Guayabo National Monument *(CR's premier archeological site)*
- Braulio Carrillo National Park
- Chirripó National Park
- Cerro Chirripó
- Birding with endemic species found no where else in the world
- Hiking
- Orosí Valley, Cachí Reservoir
- Hot Springs in Orosí & Chirripó
- Whitewater rafting / kayaking in the Reventaz
- Kayaking the flat-water of Lago de Cachí
- Horseback riding in Orosí & Chirripó

Setting Options

In the Cartago province, you can choose an idyllic farm in Orosí, a riverside or mountain home along Cerro de Muerto or simple town living in Cartago city. If you are looking for an urban draw, a business/entrepreneur region, or a social hub, this is not the province for you.

Proximity to Airport

Cartago City is approximately 1.25 hours drive to SJO international airport. Orosí will take on 15 more minutes, Turrialba 25 more for a grand total of almost 2 hours.

Social Offerings

While expats do reside in the mountains and are sparsely scattered across the cities of Cartago, as of yet there is not a large hub to exchange experiences. Spanish skills are highly recommended to be happy and social in the province. Cross Cultural Solutions is one volunteer group to get plugged into which has a presence in Cartago.
http://www.crossculturalsolutions.org/destinations/costa-rica/cartago

SAN JOSÉ

- Population: 1,404,172
- Most populated
- Largest Public Transit Hub
- Largest shopping hub
- Easy access to mountains and volcanos
- Huge Expat Community

San José is the work force of Costa Rica bringing more than a million people daily to city center for work. San José is packed with people, shops, merchandise, food, taxis, buses, and a busy industrial feel. While the city is cloaked by a blanket of business, the escape to nearby tranquil mountains, volcanoes, and valleys is often only a 20 minute drive. Many expats choose to live in the posh town of Escazú because of it's proximity to San José, the international airport (SJO), and the best schools in the country. While San José, the city, is only a small portion of the province, make certain that you are well versed in the traffic regulations enforced in the city. Because of the congestion, there are driving restrictions Monday through Friday during rush hour depending on the last number of your placa (license plate). See more in the **_Driving in Costa Rica_** section.

The government has also reopened the train lines, slowly adding more in and around San José in an attempt to relieve congestion. The train schedule can be found here:
http://www.horariodetren.com/EN/cr/

ESCAZÚ

From Escazú, you are only 15 minutes from San José, 40 minutes from the SJO airport, 10 minutes from Santa Ana, and 1.5 hours from great beaches on the Central Pacific Coast.

There is a huge range in real estate here. You can choose from posh mansions, 35 year old remodeled homes, modern condominiums, gated communities, and Tico-styled homes. There are numerous bi-lingual private school options, and CIMA, a private hospital known to provide the best care in CR, is located in town.

As far as shopping goes, Escazú has everything from restaurants, numerous grocery options, EPA *(home depot equivalent)*, banks, movie theaters, and malls! They even have Walmart and Pricemart! What more could you need?

SANTA ANA

Santa Ana is a popular suburb housing approximately 11,000 people. There is a blend of old and new in this town with a heavy history in pottery and ceramics. A church dating to 1870. New condos, gated communities, restaurants (even an Applebee's), and malls are popping up left and right. The development of the town has been so quick, the infrastructure hasn't been able to keep up. If you approach Santa Ana during rush hour, be prepared to creep at a snail's pace through the two-lane road that crosses the town.

The location is right off the newly created highway 27 with easy access to beaches, downtown and the airport.

CANGREJA NATIONAL PARK

Located in Puriscal, this relatively small park is home to more birds and flora than the more popular Corcovado National Park. It is the last virgin forest in the region. There are over 2000 plant species!

W   A   S   P   S

Weather

- As part of the Central Valley, the province boasts some of the best weather in the world!
- The actual degree depends on the elevation where you decide to settle. At 3280 ft (1,000m), average highs are 71 degrees F (22 C) and lows are 64 degrees F (18C). At 6070 feet (1850m), highs come in at 62 degrees F (17.4 C) and lows are recorded at 53 degrees F (12 C).
- Rainfall can vary from 77 inches (1960mm) to 127 inches (3230mm) depending on your location
- During the wet season, mornings are usually dry and sunny but rain creeps in during the mid-late afternoon.

Activities/Amenities

- Hiking
- Gym/Sports teams
- Social Meetups
- Shopping
- Walking

Setting Options

- Resort living
- Mountain living
- Gated communities
- Condos
- Humble homes

Proximity to Airport

Depending on your location in the province, the drive time to SJO will average approximately 30-50 minutes.

Social Offerings

Suburbs of the San José region are home to the largest expat communities in CR, especially Escazú. There are events and socials planned every day. No lack of social interaction here!

PUNTARENAS

- Population: 410,929
- Ferry to Nicoya Peninsula
- Transit Hub
- Only Pacific Port
- Largest geographic province
- Manuel Antonio, Monteverde, Carara, & Corcovado National Parks
- Tárcoles river

Puntarenas, or *"punta arenas,"* means sand point. A great representation since the majority of the region is coastal. It's the California of Costa Rica, home to loads of excellent surf spots! In addition to endless barrels, the province is host to: expansive beaches, Jaco, and magical Manuel Antonio. Caldera, the sole Pacific port, is located in Puntarenas as is the ferry that transports it's passengers, their cars, buses, and shuttles to the southern Nicoya Peninsula.

Some of the most gorgeous beaches in the country are located in this region. The beaches of Manuel Antonio, and islands Playa Naranjo, Isla Tortuga, Playa del Mal País, Jesuíta, and San Lucas are great examples.

Puntarenas is also the largest city on the Pacific, serving as a mini-San José by offering ancillary government services so that you don't have to venture all the way to San José which is a 2-4 hour drive from much of the coast.

JACO

The best way I can describe Jaco is a touristy party town with a hot night life and an even hotter surfing hub complete with hookers galore. As mentioned in the Basics, prostitution is legal and regulated in Costa Rica, and it shows in Jaco. Once the sun goes down, the stilettos come out! During the day, Jaco is a tourist mecca with exotic tour options including: waterfall rappelling, cliff diving (www.CostaRicaWaterfallTours.com), a Jet boat rides, monkey mangrove tours, zip-lining, bungee jumping, crocodile tours, and horseback riding!

Food options are vast in Jaco! Sushi, pizza, fried chicken, sandwiches, smoothies, ice cream, vegetarian, Jamaican, surf & turf, Tico food, and more! There is also a small movie theater and an american style grocery store!

There are plenty of suburbs just outside of Jaco like Herradura that offer a more relaxed way of living and are less touristy but close enough to amenities to allow you to dip into the crazy every now and then.

MANUEL ANTONIO

Manuel Antonio is the most visited park in Costa Rica for a reason! In one day you can see: monkeys, sloths, boa constrictors, toucans, numerous lizards, spiders, halloween crabs, bats, and more if you're lucky! If you go with a guide, you are often guaranteed to see a sloth!

The beach is often crowded with sticky handed capuchin, or white-faced monkeys. They are adorable, and will steal anything they can get their hands on. I watched one snatch a bottle of sunscreen out of a beachgoer's bag and sprint up a tree to investigate his find.

The beaches and scuba diving in the National Park are some of the finest in the country. Make sure to wear a swimsuit when visiting the park. Unless you plan on going off the main trek into extensive hikes, I recommend you wear flip-flops and a hat, bring a beach towel, and apply gobs of sunscreen. The main trail is wide, partially paved, and easy to navigate. Also, bring lots of water because once you are inside the park, there are no vendors.

The town of Manuel Antonio is charming, posh, hip, and expensive! The area is cut into a gorgeous mountain so everyone has a million dollar view! The restaurants are delicious but expensive, and there is an active night life. The only gay/lesbian nightclub on the pacific coast, Liquid, is located here. Did I mention it's expensive?

There are gated communities in and around Manuel Antonio. Expect them to be pricy but gorgeous.

The nearby town, Quepos, is a frugal economic option with more practical amenities and is slightly less touristy. Quepos hosts the best farmers' market in the region on Friday night and Saturday morning and is home to the main fishing port south of Puntarenas city. Scuba trips to Manuel Antonio depart from here.

DOMINICAL/ UVITA

Dominical and Uvita are rapidly becoming popular expat destinations ever since the government paved the costiñera (A Costa Rican Pacific Coast Highway). Along the Central Pacific Coast, the drive to Dominical and Uvita is very easy and pleasant. Dominical is a surf town through and through. You are likely to find more blue eyed gringos than Ticos here. This was a bit of a turn off for me since I wanted to bask in the Tico culture, but it may be just what you're looking for. The surf vibe is chill, the food is great, and there are numerous open air surf shacks along the beach to sip a beer and down a burger while checking out the building swell. Dominical does have a bit of a reputation for partying, marijuana, and more recently, cocaine use. Like anywhere the people that you surround yourself with determine if this affects you.

Uvita is just south of Dominical and boasts gorgeous empty beaches. There isn't a party scene here and practically no amenities. You will have to trek into Dominical or further for entertainment options. If you are looking for pristine jungle meets beach, you will find it in Uvita. The trade off may be a sketchy internet connection and occasionally poor water service to your home *(depending on how your home gets it's water)*.

Make sure and ask your landlord or real estate agent about water service in this area. If the property you choose has its own well water, you might bypass the problem altogether.

The region is unarguably gorgeous! There is a beach in the Marino Ballena National Park that has a sandbar that literally forms a whales tale! In the recent past you could walk out on the tail during low tide but the sandbar was damaged after the Japanese tsunami on March 11th, 2011. Now you have to swim out to it. But it's still partially visible at low tide from an areal view. The park is named after the humpback whales that migrate here every year from December to April to get frisky before returning to the frigid waters in the north.

MONTEVERDE CLOUD FOREST RESERVE

Breathtaking... You really are among the clouds in this idyllic eden. The town of Monteverde is small and geared towards tourists. The frog and snake museum is not to be missed! There are a variety of suspension bridges and zip lines to experience the cloud forest from a monkey's view at the tree tops. The prized quetzal bird is often spotted in Monteverde, along with numerous other species. I attended an excellent Spanish school, CPI, in the center of town while I was exploring Monteverde. They offer private and group lessons along with nearby home stays. I was placed with an excellent host family that patiently helped me work on my Spanish and cooked delicious Tico food for me. I had my own room and bathroom, and could walk uphill to school. I was part of a group lesson of 3 people and learned more Spanish in that week than I did in all of my high school Spanish classes combined.

As far as living in the area, there aren't many amenities, and the road to get to Monteverde is riddled with pot holes. Access is difficult and tiresome. There are plans to pave the road in the near future which will be great for those who wish to visit and live in the region. However, I am wary that the Monteverde of today will never be seen again once better access is achieved.

CORCOVADO NATIONAL PARK

The most isolated national park in Costa Rica, is Corcovado National Park, also known as the amazon of Costa Rica. It is home to the largest primary forest in all of the Americas along the pacific! The park is home to eight habitats, more than 400 species of birds, 116 reptiles and amphibians, and 139 different mammals. There are more scarlet macaws here than any other spot in Costa Rica. Tapirs and big cats rule the region. Corcovado also has more Jaguars sightings than anywhere else in the country.

W A S P S

Weather

- Puntarenas, as a primarily coastal province is one of the warmer regions of Costa Rica, ranging from sunny and 86 degrees to a squelching 96 degrees!
- Rain can vary from 59 - 197 inches (1500mm to 5000mm) annually

Activities/Amenities

- Surfing
- Hiking
- Birding
- Waterfall frolicking and rappelling
- Walking
- Cliff diving
- Romantic sunset dinners

Setting Options

- Condos
- Gated Communities
- Stand alone houses
- Posh homes on a cliff with Pacific views
- Tico-style homes
- Mountain Living
- Costal surf shacks

Proximity to Airport

It's going to be a bit of a trek from the Puntarenas province to the airport. Depending on where you live, you are looking at a 1-4 hour drive to SJO. There is an option to fly with Sansa or Nature Air to Quepos from San José (Pavas for Nature Air, SJO for Sansa). For the Domincal and Uvita folks, that shaves off at least 2.5 hours leaving them with a 1 to 1.5 hour drive from the Quepos landing strip.

Social Offerings

In Jaco and Dominical, expats abound! Smaller towns like Esterillos exude the small town feel with a Tico spin. Uvita is fairly isolated with Domincal being the nearest extrovert outlet. For those who venture to the Osa Peninsula, they are off of the grid completely!

TRY BEFORE YOU PRY

HOW RENTING PRIOR TO BUYING IN YOUR DESIRED LOCATION CAN SAVE YOU BUCKET LOADS

In my "last life," I was a paramedic. In the emergency medical field, the mantra "Try before you pry" was a common and important one. When we approach a residence or car at an accident, we always attempt to gain entry by turning the handle before we break the door down.

Try it on

Costa Rica is intoxicating which is why after a brief visit, many people find themselves snatching up property while wearing "tourist goggles." Buying a house or property in Costa Rica should *NEVER* be done on a whim.

Mike Marino, owner of a Costa Rican Tour company, said *"I can always tell how long a tourist has been in town by their questions Fresh off the plane they ask, 'You live here? Why did you leave the United States?' After about five days to one week exploring the country, they ask what are the schools like and how expensive is it to live here?"* It doesn't take long to drink the *pura vida* Kool-aide!

First off, you might get ripped off if you don't do your homework. Second, you are viewing CR from your vacation/tourist goggles. You need to live in your desired region for at least six months, but a year would be better. While renting a property, you can evaluate the area as a local and see what it's like after the honeymoon is over. Then, and only then, can you make a fully informed decision.

More often than not, those that leave Costa Rica with discouragement and contempt for the country are those who didn't do their homework. Their expectations did not reflect the life that Costa Rica provides.

Certainly, there are times when you perform all of your due diligence and Costa Rica is just not the right fit for you. Many more times however, people make the romantic leap into a tropical paradise without researching what exactly it entails. I can guarantee you it won't be a tropical version of your hometown.

Research online as much as you'd like, but I dare to declare that it doesn't amount to much until you forge through the country and experience real life amid the troop-less patriots.

Every industry functions differently from your hometown. You won't know if the differences are crucial to you until you experience them. After which you can decide for yourself.

Rona is a property manager in the small town on the Central Pacific Coast. She shared with me that 9 out of 10 clients that sign a lease sight unseen are less happy and more likely to break their lease. Not because the apartment or house was sub par, but because life in Costa Rica looked better to them from the travel channel.

I enthusiastically urge you to budget a trip to explore different regions and try them by renting. That way, when you do decide which region is your slice of heaven, you can sit easy knowing you have explored the country and your property is not only great but better than all of the other good options you explored.

If you think that trekking around the country is not worth the cost or time, think about the added stress and cost of selling the house you regretfully purchased. Two years on the market is a common timespan in CR.

If you have an opportunity to rent the property you are considering purchasing then all the better! You can see if the house is well built or problematic. If someone else places a bid on the property you would be given the opportunity to offer a bid of your own if you felt so inclined. A true win-win!

RENT

The benefits from renting are numerous!

Try out the area with little to no commitment.

Little financial investment, usually only requiring a deposit and first month's rent.

Peace of mind that if something breaks, and in humid CR it always does, you are not the one footing the bill. *Most houses that have AC have separate units in each room. Each unit costs around $800 to replace and often all it takes is one curious gecko to fry it.*

If you don't like your residence, or community; or family circumstances no longer allow you to stay, you can pick up and leave.

If the property proves to be a lemon, you can leave.

If you are sensitive to the energy of a place, you can try it on and decide if you thrive there.

BUY

The benefit of owning include:

- Continuity
- You are free to create your customized oasis
- Potential path for immigration (+/= $200K).
- You have potential rental income
- You can personalize the heck out of your house
- A chance to gain equity if the value rises (the chance of losing value is also present)
- Often a lower monthly housing expense that is fixed and could be paid off over time

I read about a couple that spent their savings on a house in CR without laying eyes on the property. They were happy initially but soon things became to fall apart.

In the first year, they discovered someone was stealing electricity from them and could not get help to resolve the situation. The new appliances that were purchased for the home blew during a surge from a storm! Then, after an ATM refused to provide the money that was successfully deducted from their account, the couple decided that they had had enough.

They placed the house on the market and waited. After a year, the couple decided to cut their $100K loss and walk away.

Take home message here? *Try before you pry* and your cost of living will not include a $100K debt!!

COST OF LIVING

THIS SECTION HAS BEEN STRESS TESTED BY EXPATS TODAY! ALSO INCLUDED IS A BUDGET THAT YOU CAN START WITH!

Cost of living all depends on what kind of "living" you desire. No matter your lifestyle, the corresponding cost will be less in the mountains than on the beach. You also gain money in your budget if you choose to live off of the beaten path. What you give up in convenience and access to public works, you gain back in your wallet.

I will provide my budget as an example of one way to live. I rent a condo on the Central Pacific Coast that is 400 feet from an expansive beach. The property is in a gated community with security around the clock and a private pool. I have 2 master suites and a guest bathroom downstairs. It is an open concept modern home with granite, travertine, and slate throughout. It is fully furnished including a large flat screen

TV! It has a laundry room with W/D, and even a private tiki hut in the back with a built in travertine wet bar and a propane grill including a beer fridge! It also has a covered carport that is attached to the tiki hut.

MY MONTHLY EXPENSES:

Rent: $850

Water bill: $10-15

Electric Bill: $200-210 (*I use the AC a lot!*)

Cell Phone: $20-30

Diesel Fuel: $100 (*If I don't take any long road trips*)

Car Repairs: $20 (*I have an old car*)

Groceries: $250

Drinks out: $20 (*I don't go out much*)

Cable Internet/TV: $60 (*I am two levels above the basic for faster internet downloading/uploading*)

_____

Monthly total= $1,545

You will notice that I don't include eating out or much social spending calculated in so make appropriate changes. Also, if you want a larger property or one that has the sand at your front door, tweak the budget accordingly.

HOUSING

Make a list of your must haves and your highly desired qualities in a home. Do you want little to no upkeep, to live in a gated community, or resort community? Are you looking for a farm with fruit trees and a garden? Do you want to live among other expats or fully integrate with Ticos? What type of lease are you looking for?

Keep in mind that some communities are geared for the part time expat so features and security may vary according to the season. It is very likely that your neighbors will also fluctuate since many expats only live abroad part time and others decide it's not for them. Depending on your personality, and if your Spanish is not so good, you will either want to immerse yourself in the Tico community to learn the language or hideaway in a "gringo-land" of your choosing.

RENT

There is an outstanding market for rental homes in CR. You can rent anything from a multi-million dollar mansion that overlooks the Pacific to a humble Tico-styled cabina in the mountains while paying anything from $250 to $3,000 per month!

Make sure to find out if there are AC units in each room, central air, or fans only. Central air is nice but will hike up your utility bills since you are cooling the entire house instead of just the room that you are in. At the time, see if you can get the utilities included in your rent. This makes for a simplistic rental experience when you don't have to set up a new account with cabletica for your internet or hunt down the water company to pay your $8.00 bill.

Below are a few examples of rentals on the market on the date this book was written:

✱ A 3 bedroom / 3.5 bathroom, office, 2 car garage, granite, american style, 300 meters to the country club, maid's quarters with full bath, 3800 ft^2 rental in Escazú (Posh suburb of San José) will run you **$2,500** per month.

✱ A 3 bedroom, 2 bath house in the modern gated community of El Guarco, Cartago, comes fully furnished with a 2 car garage, patio, mountain views, 2200 ft^2, security 24/7, 10 mins from downtown Cartago, and 30 mins from San José **$550** per month.

✳ A 2 bedroom / 2 bathroom upscale fully furnished condo in Tamarindo. Granite, breakfast bar, open concept great room, ranchos with BBQ, 3 huge pools, multiple flat screens, 24/7 security, carport, close to numerous beaches, **$800** per month

✳ A 2 bedroom / 1 bathroom furnished apartment in Cocles, Puerto Viejo. Fast internet, the property has its own well so it's never out of water, short walking distance to a gorgeous white sand beach that is great for surfing, a gorgeous handmade wooden deck equipped with a hammock. **$650** per month plus utilities.

PURCHASING A PROPERTY

Make sure you read the ***Try Before You Pry*** section before you proceed to this section.

If you have constructed a home in the United States then you are familiar with how many details are required to make a quality home. Add to that zero regulation, a language barrier, no clear contractor licensure, a confusing permit process, Tico time, and you have Costa Rican Building! On the plus side, labor is very cheap and many materials are cheaper here except plumbing and Air Conditioning parts.

There are endless lots for sale. Peruse at your leisure for your dream home location. Part of the reason there are so many lots for sale is because people make hasty purchases. Do your research, and live in the area where you want to buy before purchasing. Buying a lot is a fairly quick process, selling one can take years.

COSTA RICAN BANK LOAN

In order to apply for a loan with a Costa Rican bank, you have to be patient, well organized, and have some cash. Typically, they require *at least* a 20% downpayment, 8-13% interest rate, closing costs, 10-20 year term, and are dreadfully slow to close, taking anywhere from 6 weeks to 3 months! Take care to see if your interest rate jumps after the first 3 years, this is a common occurrence.

If you don't have a nest-egg stashed away to pay for your Tico home in cold hard cash, not to worry, you're not alone. Borrowing from Costa Rican banks is nearly impossible as an expat which is why a "work around" using owner financing was developed and has been practiced successfully for over 20 years.

OWNER FINANCING

There are a variety of different arrangements with owner-financing so make sure you are comfortable with your terms. Be careful to choose a structure that protects both the buyer and seller. A downpayment ranges from 30-50%. Interest is usually between 6-10%, and there are no pre-payment penalties with a speedy closing!

INTERNATIONAL LOAN

If you have an excellent relationship or history with your bank in your home country and are able to secure financing through them, more power to you! Take care to compare the terms, interest, and conditions of all viable options and consult your attorney (they will be well versed in the variety of owner financing arrangements possible) before you settle on one.

CLOSING COSTS

Good news! Closing costs are often shared with the seller. Once you choose the perfect property, be prepared to dole out part or all of the following closing costs:

- 1.25% for your attorney
- 1.5% in government stamps and fees if your property is already owned by a corporation, therefore you simply complete a share transfer
- 2.5% in government stamps and fees when the title needs to be changed, i.e. placing the property in your name or the name of your corporation.
- If you use a third-party escrow then they will have their own escrow fees (relatively low).
- All percentages are based on the *Declared Value* of the property which is often only 20-40% of what you spent on the home

PROPERTY & MUNICIPAL TAXES

Coming in at 0.25-1.5% of the *Declared Value* of the property, property taxes are deliciously lower than the States! Since the Declared Value is often a fraction of what you paid, you save in numerous ways!

Property taxes are collected every calendar year the local municipal government. The same group collects a general tax that covers water, sewage, and garbage pickup. Just like in North America, the amount of these services varies depending on where you live, but unlike the States, it is usually quite low.

To place it in context of real life, let's suppose you buy a killer pad for $100K USD. Your annual taxes will be around $50 USD, pura vida!

LUXURY HOME TAX

In 2009, Costa Rica added the Solidarity Tax for the Strengthening of Housing Programs *(Impuesto Solidario para el Fortalecimiento de Programs de Vivienda).*[10] The program is often referred to as the "luxury tax," since it only applies to houses with a value of over 100 million Colones *($198,526 at the time of writing).* The tax is in addition to the normal annual property taxes. Exceptions include: owning land without structures on it or your house is *valued* under $198,526.

The tax ranges from 0.25-0.55% of the *value* of the house. It is a sliding scale dependent on the value of your home. The top of the scale is for houses valued above 1.5 billion colones *(Almost 3 million USD).*

The "Luxury Tax" is due by January 15 of each year.

The program was developed to help shanty barrios throughout Costa Rica.

UTILITIES

As in any home, cost will vary depending on how large your home is, how many people reside in your home, and how they use their resources. Using the AC is one of the biggest factors in your utility bills. Many people decide to acclimate to the hot and humid weather and save cold showers for a treat. I have neighbors that don't like the AC because they don't like going from hot to cold and visa versa. I love my AC and don't plan on giving it up. See my utility costs at the beginning of *Cost of Living* Section.

As far as internet providers, some towns will not have cable options, and you will be forced to use DSL or a 3G stick. The 3G stick would cost you per MB of data transferred. In laymen's terms, the more emails, music listened to, and movies watched, the more expensive it would get.

---

[10] Law 8683

To be perfectly honest, your download speeds are so dreadfully slow, streaming anything is a joke.

FOOD

I spend about $50 bucks a week on groceries. This is one item of cost of living that can vary drastically from person to person. If you are set on eating the exact same things that you did when you lived in North America or Europe, then you could easily double or triple this cost because all your food would have to be imported. It can also double depending on your drinking habits.

Shopping at farmers markets for your produce for the week saves you many colones!   Unfortunately, cheese has gotten out of hand. The cost of a bag of shredded mozzarella can run you $8 bones! You can get an entire pizza for eight dollars in the States! Other expensive items include name brand laundry detergent like Tide or All, chocolate, and cereal. If you eat like a Tico: rice, beans, fresh fruit and vegetables, juice, and water, you could spend far less than my estimated $50 a week.

TRANSPORTATION

BUS

There is a bus to get you just about anywhere in Costa Rica you desire. They are cheap, relatively clean, and run you about $1 per hour of driving. Try to bring change as it is often hard for the driver to break a large bill.

There are numerous public and private operators with varying degrees of comfort offered. For the longer distance buses, AC and bathrooms are often utilized. For most local jaunts, the buses are older and sport open air concepts of comfort.

Vendors will often pop on board and sell you mangos, fresh juices, popsicles, water, agua de pipa (coconut water), and more for mere pennies.

TAXI

Taxis are safe and plentiful in the larger cities and near tourist attractions. If you are off the beaten path, it is usually still possible to get a cab by asking the restaurant or hotel to call one. It is always best to only accept rides in marked taxis. Make sure to negotiate the rate before you get into the car. A two hour cab ride will run you anywhere from $100-150 depending on your negotiating skills in Spanish and how busy the day has been for your driver. Short runs around town will cost you a few dollars.

VEHICLE COSTS
- Cost to Ship, Import Taxes
- Initial Purchase
- Fuel
- Marchamo
- RITEVE
- Repairs

Shipping your car will easily run you from $1500-2000 USD. Import taxes will likely be about 50-60% of your car's value. See the *Shipping Your Car* section for more info.

Purchasing a car in Costa Rica is not cheap. To get a quality vehicle that is less than 10 years old, expect to pay at least $12,000. Most likely you will pay more! I paid $7,000 for a 1980 CJ7 Diesel Jeep. Diesel engines are desired because they get better fuel efficiency, are supposed to climb hills better, and diesel fuel is cheaper than gas here. See more about how to buy a car and what to look for in a CR car in the *After You Arrive* section.

The fuel prices are regulated by the government and are a pretty penny. According to the government's last price hike on March 21st, 2013: one liter will run you $1.44 USD or $5.45 per gallon for the cheap stuff! Diesel is $1.28 per liter or $4.85 per gallon.

Marchamo is the Costa Rican equivalent to paying your tags, taxes, and car insurance all in one stop due on 12/31 every year for everyone. The amount that you pay is based predominantly on the make and age of the car.

The insurance is provided through the National Insurance Institute (INS) and is built into your Marchamo fee. It only costs $49.92 for the obligatory insurance which covers up to $12,000 in victim's accident and medical expenses as of the controversial 2013 increase.

If you are looking into purchasing a car and are curious how much the Marchamo will cost text message 1467 with the word Marchamo and the car's license plate number (placa).

To pay your Marchamo, simply visit any bank or INS office, or pay online at www.ins-cr.com

RITEVE is a vehicle safety inspection conducted every year on every vehicle. When it's conducted is based on the last number of your license plate, or placa. If it ends in a 1, your Reteve is due in January, a 2 February, and so on. Depending on the age of your car, this can be a simple or complex procedure. They look for excessive rust and functioning lights, turn signals, breaks, horn, windshield wipers, doors, speedometer, gas cap that fits, bumpers attached correctly, visible and lit license plate, muffler and emission control, decent tires, and so on. RITEVE approved mechanics are easily found throughout the country. To find the nearest location go to: http://rtv.co.cr. Take care to visit a reputable shop and it's best to use a referral. Otherwise, your gringo-hood might cost a repair or two. If you have a Tico/Tica friend, see if they would take your car in for you.

EXPERIENCE

We piled 7 people into our Toyota 4 Runner for an adventure at a local waterfall. We had two other packed cars caravanning with us, and when we arrived at the falls there was three other cars already there. We hiked into the falls (about a 10 minute walk) and started about our day enjoying the sun, water, and beer! After we had been there about 30 minutes, a torrential rainfall started out of nowhere! Some people screamed and ran for shelter. Others just laughed and tried to keep the rain out of their beers. The water level at the falls began to rise. It was clearly time to go, so we slugged our way back through the fields to our cars. All 5 cars got stuck in the flooded clay. None of us had cell phone service on this mountain, and we really had no idea how to resolve the situation. After about 30 minutes, a Tico on a tractor slowly approached us. All 20-25 of us starting whistling and heeling and hawing. The Tico wore a huge grin and laughed with us. He rescued all 7 cars, one by one, attaching a chain to the chassis and towing them down the hill like little toys to where the road was drivable. After he was done, we all gathered around to collect tips for his time, service, and help. He adamantly refused, and said that he was just glad that he could help (this was all in Spanish of course).

~ Mikey & Diana, Managers at Hotel Encantada
www.EncantadaCostaRica.com

Repairs are inevitable. Between thick clay, bumpy roads, and humidity, something is bound to fail. Electrical systems are incessantly difficult to manage. That is why it's good to try and purchase a car with as few electrical components as possible. If your car is newer or more specialized, it will cost more to repair. My mechanical problems are usually a loose or broken wire but have included brake issues, my drive shaft falling out, and a wheel falling off while driving! Most repairs were between $10-40. If you need a mechanic near Parrita, *Multiservicios Montero* (green sign) is an excellent option, Spanish speaking only. See the *Resource Directory* at the end of the book for more mechanics.

DOMESTIC HELP

If you are simply looking for someone to clean your home once a week or once a month, then you can hire a maid for the day. If you are looking for full-time help, then you must abide by labor laws specified by CAJA.[11] You will pay around $300 a month for a live out full time maid, and $150 for a live in with room and board included. If you are paying them for the day, the rate varies from $10-20.

My home could be scrubbed in less than 4 hours and I paid $20 because Patricia, my housecleaner, did an excellent job and was extremely trustworthy. I want her to be happy so I can continue to invite her into my home without concern over my belongings. Referrals are important when you are inviting strangers into your space whether in the States or in CR. Remember, your belongings are often worth enough to pay their wages for years. Make sure that you keep them happy! If they are cleaning all day, cook a little extra lunch and dinner to share with them. Invite them to eat with you and take a break. Get to know them and practice your Spanish!

MEDICAL CARE

Costa Rica was recently rated as the top "Medical Tourism" destination for it's low cost, high quality health care. Each person's needs, will of course, vary the cost in their budget, however, I can tell you that. Your monthly CAJA payment (insurance) varies depending on your age. Paul Ford, mentioned in the *Healthcare* section, is greater than 59 years of age and only pays $708 per year for himself, his partner, and her child. This included free doctors visits, medicines, emergency coverage, and even some dental!

---

[11] Some rules include: 2 week notice of discontinuation, paid severance, half-day holidays, ≤12 hour of work per day with a 1 hour lunch break; see Chapter VIII Articles 101- 108 of the Labor Code.

MEDICATION

Costa Rica doesn't have the pharmaceutical giants setting ungodly prices for medicines that are supposed to help us. This results in many affordable medications. There are some medicines that are only made in the States and Europe, and thereby are imported resulting in a higher cost. If you subscribe to CAJA, many medications are included in your modest fee. If you are paying as you go, the expense will vary dramatically based on how many medications you take.

PART III

LOGISTICS

FROM THEORETICAL TO UNPACKING YOUR SUITCASE

BEFORE YOU ARRIVE

Think back to the last time you moved. Take a few deep breaths, I'm sorry to bring back such a horrific memory. Indeed, moving is stressful! In order to minimize stress, cost, and errors, organization is essential. Now imagine moving to another country with customs, passports, visas, immigration paperwork, and your stuff!

Not to worry, hundreds of people including myself have done this before and we are going to get you organized in the following pages. Keep an eye out for check lists throughout the section.

SQUARE UP DEBTS

Living abroad is infinitely more possible and manageable without debt. The heaviest anvils weighing you down are your credit card and school loan debts.

Create a new budget and ditch as many "wants" as you can, leaving only your needs. Moving to Costa Rica is now your biggest want, so keep that in mind when you sacrifice small things like HBO or cable all together.

In addition to ditching cable, start brown bagging again, thereby eating out less. Look at what you are eating. Almost every Tico meal includes rice and beans in one form or another. Start eating like a Tico and loose weight while increasing your balance in your checking account!

If you decide to sell your car rather than ship it (and I'll bet that will be the right choice for you), use the money to pay off credit card debt. Costa Rica has excellent public transit and is pedestrian friendly. You can save up for another car after you arrive.

Retire Happy by Richard Stim and Ralph Warner has some other great tips on how to convert debt into retirement savings.

SECURE DOCUMENTS

After reading the **Immigration** section, if you qualify for a cedula then make sure to secure all the paperwork needed Stateside before your departure. This will save months of frustration and hundreds of dollars.[12]

If your driver's license or passport are going to expire soon, make sure and renew them in advance so they arrive before you depart! If you have children, make sure their passports will arrive well before your departure.

---

[12] see Immigration for more information on required paperwork

FOUR LEGGED FRIENDS

Bringing pets into Costa Rica is a fairly easy process. There is no quarantine period if you bring your pet like luggage. If you have them imported as freight, you may be subject to customs charges and a hold time.

Make sure you are well versed in your airline's pet transport policy before you purchase your ticket! Some airlines restrict weight limits for in-cabin pets. Other restrictions often include maximum outdoor temperature and nonstop flights only.

If you need a starting place, review the pet policies of the airlines in *Pet Policies*.

Upon entrance to Costa Rica you will need the following documents:

☐ A pet health certificate issued within 10 days of travel by your vet in the country of origin

☐ Dogs: proof of vaccination against distemper, hepatitis, parovirus (DHLPP), leptospirosis, coronavirus, parainfluenza, and rabies

☐ Cats: feline viral rhinotrachetis, panleukopenia (FVRCP), calicivirus, and rabies

☐ All vaccines except rabies must be administered *within 30 days* of departure to CR

☐ Rabies vaccines must be given *more than 30 days* but less than *12 months* prior to traveling to CR. The three-year rabies vaccine is not recognized in CR.

PET POLICIES

United:
http://www.united.com/web/en-us/content/travel/animals/default.aspx

American:

http://www.aa.com/i18n/travelInformation/specialAssistance/travelingWithPets.jsp

Frontier:

http://www.flyfrontier.com/customer-service/travel-support/family-pets/traveling-with-pets

Jet Blue:

http://www.jetblue.com/travel/pets/

Delta:

http://www.delta.com/content/www/en_US/traveling-with-us/special-travel-needs/pets/pet-requirements-restrictions.html

US Airways:

http://www.usairways.com/en-US/traveltools/specialneeds/pets.html

Spirit:

http://spirit.zendesk.com/entries/21368453-Can-I-bring-my-pet-with-me-

There are a few ways to get your loved four-legger to CR. If they are small, you can carry them on in a carrier for a fee with most airlines. Make sure you read the actual airline's policy (the included links) and not a third party's site. During the research for this book, there were numerous out-of-date sources of information. For example, Frontier cancelled their shipment of pets as cargo (checked pets) on 11/1/12, but most sites still listed their old policy. The last thing you want when showing up for your flight and to be surprised.

If you have a service dog or therapy dog, they can board with you with the proper identification without a fee. If your pet is not a service dog, nor do they fit under the seat in a carrier, then your options are restricted to shipping them in the belly of the plane or hiring a pet transporter to ship them.

Pet transportation companies utilize smaller planes that are temperature regulated. They also often include a vet tech, or other caretaker to monitor your furry children assuring that they remain calm and sedated as necessary.

Services like Pet Movers are pricey but can actually deliver your pet door to door! They also provide you with a moving counselor who will help facilitate the best schedule and route so that your pet has the fewest connections possible. They provide the kennels used during transit, kenneling when necessary for customs, shots and paperwork as needed, and obtain international import permits! They are also a member of the IPATA and USDA pet handlers. http://www.petmovers.com/services/

Shop around and find the best pet transporter that fits your budget and requirements. There are many of scammers in the transportation sector. I recommend visiting www.ipata.org to shop for your transporter. Only reputable pet transporters are awarded certification through the International Pet and Animal Transportation Association (IPATA). The website also includes information on airlines, insurance, vets, animal handlers and more!

MAIL SYSTEM

You need to reshape your mail to suit your international living.
☐ Make sure you unsubscribe from magazines, catalogs, and other snail mail subscriptions.
☐ Start a list now of people and companies that you will need to advise of your move. You may believe there are only 10 or 15 people, but I bet that as time progresses, you will think of more and more businesses, friends, and services that need to know you are moving.

☐Set up online billing and statements for your bank, credit card company, student loans, etc.

☐Sign up for an absentee ballot if you are interested in keeping up with your rights as a US citizen

☐If you have family that is extremely supportive and want to lend a hand, ask them to use their address as your US address and have them email you pictures of your mail as it comes in. This favor will require occasional shipping of mail and packages to you.

☐Or invest in a mail service that will provide at least one US address, scan pictures of your mail and allow you to respond with options to trash or ship to you: (Aerocasillas, Mailboxes Etc, JetBox, Jetex, Star Box)

BANKING

Your local credit union was an excellent choice for you in your hometown, but as an international bank it might fall short. Re-evaluate your current bank with the following criteria designed to suit your new life as an expat.

●Can you fax a wire request to transfer money?

●Are there ATM fees, if so are they excessive?

●What is the currency transaction fee?

●If you are receiving a pension, Social Security, or annuity, can the payments be automatically deposited to your current bank? (www.ssa.gov/foreign/index.html)

●Do they offer mobile deposits?

●Are they FDIC insured?

●Is there a minimum balance requirement to avoid maintenance fees?

Most banks charge a foreign transaction fee (a percentage of your purchase) each time that you swipe your debit card for a bill that is in a currency other than that of your country of origin. For example, if your bank charges a 10% currency transaction fee (CTF) and you buy dinner for $35 USD, your currency transaction fee will be $3.50 USD! CTFs add up quickly as do ATM fees.

I didn't think to change banks before I moved to CR. In just 6 months of living in Costa Rica, I racked up $210.67 USD in fees just to access my money! I now proudly bank with Charles Schwab and pay zero fees *(information to follow)*.

Many places in Costa Rica are cash driven. Some small towns don't even have a bank or ATM. Where I live, I drive 20 mins to get to an ATM. Other towns require a trek of over an hour to access money from an ATM. As cash is becoming obsolete in the US, it still is a commodity in CR. Most tourist towns will accept the US dollar, but if you venture off the beaten path, you may run into resistance.

Check to see what your bank charges each time you access your money from an "out of network" ATM. More often than not, the bank whose ATM you are using will also apply a fee. You could be looking at anywhere between $5-10 USD just to use the ATM! If you are withdrawing Colones instead of US Dollars, tack on the Foreign Transaction Fee.

You might conclude that your bank will not serve you well as an international resource. I have banked with Bank of America, Washington Mutual, and most recently Wells Fargo. I was paying way to much to access my money internationally, so I did some research and found a bank that offers everything I was looking for. Charles Schwab's High Yield Investor's Checking Account. *(I do not receive any kickbacks from CS but would love if you mentioned who sent you to them)*

Take a look at the benefits:

☑ Zero maintenance fees

☑ Zero minimum balance requirement

☑ ZERO CURRENCY TRANSACTION FEES

☑ Free brokerage account

☑ Mobile deposits

☑ Online banking

☑ UNLIMITED ATM FEE REIMBURSEMENTS- not only do they not charge ATM fees of their own, they take it one step further and reimburse you for the fees other banks charge to use their ATMs to access your money around the world!

CREDIT CARDS

It is a good idea to have one or two credit cards for emergencies. If you already have your favorite credit cards, make sure they do not expire anytime soon.

Every time I travel at least one of my cards gets turned off due to a fraud alert. Even when I call ahead of time and tell my bank my travel plans. Having your cards turned off can be detrimental, which is why I always have three cards. I maintain two credit cards and one debit card, but I never keep all three on my person. I prefer to keep one credit card at home just in case I were to loose or have my wallet taken from me.

As with your bank, you need to asses your current cards. Do they serve you? I prefer to use credit cards that give me travel rewards and little or no currency transaction fees. Since I travel internationally, I look for airlines that go to the countries I plan to visit, i.e. American Airlines (One World Alliance) and United (Star Alliance).

If your credit is decent, the *Chase Sapphire Preferred card* might be a good fit. There are a variety of ways to earn points and each point can easily be transferred to any airline program point for mile. It's pretty nice to have that kind of flexibility. Another option is the AAdvantage card offered through Citi Bank in conjunction with American Airlines. I have never enjoyed working with Citi, but I will say it is very easy redeem your miles anytime on flights around the world. I have flown no fewer than 7 times with this card. The longest flight was from Santiago, Chile to Kansas City, USA. I paid $80 in taxes and fuel surcharge and used 30,000 miles! If you have to make a purchase, you might as well make it work for you!

TIP
Pay attention to additional ways to earn miles. For example, AAdvantage has a dining club you can easily join for free. Once you are a member, you can search for restaurants in your area that participate in the dining club. Each time you dine at a participating restaurant, you accumulate between 3-5 times the miles per dollar spent! It doesn't take long for the points to rack up! Also, they will send an email when they are running additional promotions. I recently received over 1,000 miles just for clicking the button in my email to sign up for a promotion that allowed me to gain 750 miles by dining twice over summer!

ALL OF YOUR CRAP

Our belongings can cause a great deal of stress If not dealt with correctly. The first three questions you must ask yourself are: What do I need to take with me? What select items do I want to ship? Would it make more sense to buy new furnishings or send my houseful in a container?

Take a mental inventory of everything you have in your house. Out of everything in your cupboards, closets, and drawers, how much of it do you actually use on a regular basis? Many people are "collectors" with big houses to fill. Just because you own it does not mean you need to ship it. The hardest decision about moving your belongings is whether to sell or donate everything and start anew, or rent a container, ship your stuff and deal with taxes and customs on the flip side.

STARTING FRESH

New life with new stuff

You don't end up paying large taxes on stuff you already bought

No waiting months for your belongings, just go out and shop for your house contents

Spring cleaning

Your house decor will be authentic Costa Rican furnishings

Selling provides a nice chunk of change to help with moving expenses

Most of the time it is cheaper to sell and replace than to ship

If starting fresh is your route allow for a few weeks or months to sell or donate everything outside of your suitcases. Conquer one room at a time, leaving the kitchen for last since you will be using kitchen items up until the move.

I'm a 6'0'' tall woman which is unheard of in CR. Besides curious stares, it translates to is difficulty finding clothes and shoes that fit. Keep that in mind while packing. Costa Rican men usually range between 5'2-5'9'' and women between 4'10''-5'5''. Craigslist, eBay, and Facebook are great resources when slimming down your belongings.

While Costa Rica has plenty of low cost furniture options, they do not have low cost options in electronics. In fact, many desired electronic devices are not available in the country.

Every situation is different. In my personal circumstance it made no sense to ship a container. I have never been attached to "stuff" outside of my electronics! I have moved regularly every 6 months - 2 years for the last 15 years so I have not accumulated stuff. The only kitchen item that I brought was a nice all purpose cooking knife (I love to cook) and a magic bullet blender. My furnished condo has everything else that I need. Your situation may however, include kids, a house full of furniture, antiques, books that you want to reference, and other items you have grown attached to and want to keep.

CONTAINER

- If you have the perfect furniture set (bedroom / living room) you don't have to part with it
- Don't have to figure out where to buy furnishings
- Often Tico furnishings are not as soft and cozy as your home furnishings
- Buy insurance for the container
- Research your moving company
- Ask expats for referrals
- Pay import duties and taxes

Take time to make this decision, it's a big one. If you decide on using a container, make sure you are prepared to wait weeks and sometimes months for your belongings. The average timeframe is 4-8 weeks.

IMPORT DUTIES & TARIFFS

The Customs Department of the Ministry of Treasury is going to want some "skin" for each item that you bring into Costa Rica. The way to decipher anticipated costs is to research the International Convention on the Harmonized

---

TIP

Consider shipping your belongings ahead of yourself
You can easily rent furniture or stay with family for a month prior to your departure to you new life as an expat. Once you arrive in Costa Rica, the culture, language, new climate, and daily life acquisitions can be exhausting! Add to that an empty house and the lack of basic necessities for 8+ weeks, and you have a recipe for a mental breakdown! In Costa Rica, there are no furniture rental options. Often times you will have a partially or fully furnished home, but it won't be *your* stuff. That is more important to some than others.

Commodity Description and Coding System (HS). A code system that was developed by the World Customs Organization (WCO). Kinda' sounds like studying the IRS rules and regulations right? Another way is to ask your mover for their best estimate of your taxes and tariffs. If they are experienced, they should be able to get you close to your actual amount.

INTERNATIONAL MOVERS

Finding the right moving company is key. A place to start the search would be International Movers www.intlmovers.com and www.moverreviews.com. The first is a brokerage company. You enter your origin and destination locations and they find companies that service your new and old areas. This allows you to request numerous quotes at once. The second web site collects hundreds of reviews for the most popular movers. Compare your quotes to the reviews, BBB, and www.movingscam.com before making a decision. Also, ask for references from each company that you are considering and call them. Question the references about any damage and how the company managed those issues. Ask if the shippers were on time and if they could track their shipment throughout the process.

RAINIER OVERSEAS MOVERS, INC.

I have read many positive reviews about Rainier, however, when it came down to contacting them they seemed overworked and understaffed. The fact that they are busy would be a good indicator but having trouble interacting with them causes me concern. They did respond quickly to an online quote however. This is what they had to say:

"The cost to spot an empty 20ft steamship container to San Diego, CA for you to load (48 hours free time), move back to the port of Long Beach, take care of all US Export documents, US port/terminal fees, and ocean freight to inland container depot in San José will be $3450 all inclusive. If you wanted to use our professional packing and loading services that would be an additional $1900- $2900, and home delivery to a San José residence would run roughly $900-$1400. Transit time: 25-39 days"

They also included several letters of recommendation from recent clients. Rainier scores an A+ with the Better Business Bureau, almost unheard of for a moving company. They're also endorsed through www.movingscam.com and are licensed through the Federal Maritime Commission, International Association of Movers, and Latin American & Caribbean Moving Association. The U.S. Department of Transportation Federal Motor Carrier Safety Administration has only two complaints one in 2006 and one in 2009.

www.rainieros.com

OCEAN STAR INTERNATIONAL, INC.

This mover maintains an A rating with the BBB and has been mentioned in Mover Mag and USA Today as one of the best moderately priced movers in the States. After requesting a quote for a move from San Diego to Costa Rica with a 3 bedroom house, I was given the following quote:

"If you are only shipping boxes, the cost will most likely range between $300-$500."

They clearly are geared to partitioned containers with other customers. This can save you in expenses but can cause additional delays because the container will most likely not ship until it is full. They then go on to offer packing services and quotes on full container loads. They request the number of boxes, list of furniture, service desired (packing, door-to-door deliver, port-to-port) for a more accurate quote. http://osishipping.com

MAYFLOWER TRANSIT, LLC

Founded in 1927, they have been around the block a time or two! They are not accredited through the Better Business Bureau as Mayflower Transit but through their parent company Unigroup.[13] Their rating is an A+ but some of the complaints didn't look like fun. I have used them personally for a domestic move, and it was professionally performed on time without damage to my property. Since they partner with a variety of different movers, I'm not sure if the consistency of service is provided across the board. www.mayflower.com

AIR 7 SEAS TRANSPORT LOGISTICS, INC.

BBB rates them with an A-. They have professional affiliations with the IATA, FIATA, CNS, and FMC. Here is the quote they provided from San Diego to San José, Costa Rica:

"Rate for shipping a 20' container door to port in San José: $3195. This price excludes Duties, taxes, tariff, transshipment charges, Destination Port storage fees, actual customs clearance, and door delivery. It

---

[13] http://www.bbb.org/stlouis/business-reviews/moving-storage-companies/unigroup-in-fenton-mo-310249204

includes 2 hours of loading time in San Diego ($85 p/hr after the initial 2 hours of loading time). "

SHIP TO COSTA RICA

Below is a detailed quote from **Ship to Costa Rica** partial owner, Charles Zeller as seen on www.joincostarica.com and directly thereafter, two testimonials of a customers who used their services:

"The self pack and load Door to Door rate from Toronto Ontario Canada to San Ramon de Tres Ríos, Costa Rica is as follows:

- *1x20 container (1050 CFT) with used household goods only is $7,315*
- *1x40 container (2250 CFT) with used household goods only is $8,835*

This door to door rate includes :
1. Placing a container at your residence (Legal parking only) and waiting 2 hours for you to load the container.
- *Each additional hour is USD $100.00*
2. Transportation to port of Exit
3. Ocean Freight to Port Costa Rica.
4. Port Charges
5. Transportation from Port to Customs in Alajuela.
6. Unload of container at Bonded warehouse 8. Customs inspection , MINAE permits, Customs Clearance.
7. IMPORT DUTIES ON ALL USED HOUSEHOLD GOODS. (Excludes duties and charges on new items and high end appliances such as LCD or Plasma TVs)
8. Loading of goods onto our trucks.
9. Delivery to residence in San Ramon de Tres Rios. (Easy access assumed)
10. Placing of the goods in their respective rooms or areas and same day removal of debris.

Rate excludes :
1. Inspection by US Customs authorities if required and the demurrage charges caused by this.
*2. Insurance. This is provided **as an option**. On Self pack shipments only limited insurance can be provided. The rate of 2.5% of the declared value.*

*QUOTES ARE GOOD FOR 30 DAYS AND SUBJECT TO CHANGES IN THE
TRANSPORTATION RATES THAT FLUCTUATE ACCORDING TO THE OIL PRICES.*

*Transit time is about 4 to 8 weeks door to door. Six is average.
Form of payment is 60 % once loaded and the rest in Costa Rica once shipment
arrives to Customs and before delivery in cash or cashier check drawn against a
local bank. Wire transfer is also possible if done ahead of time."*

Jessica and her family of 6 used Ship to Costa Rica and could not say
enough kind things about it. "It was the easiest part of our move to Costa Rica.
I arranged for the 20' container to be delivered to our house. We packed it to
the brim and they picked it up and shipped it to Costa Rica. They quoted us up
to 6 weeks. It arrived in 3 so they stored it for us since our stuff beat us there!
Then, once we were in Bejuco they delivered it to us, with two movers who
emptied the container for us. From Florida with us packing and loading it, it ran
about $5,500, but this was back in 2007." *See the Experience table on the next
page for the second review.*

EXPERIENCE

"The process was great until things went missing... The initial inventory and quote to ship our container from Salt Lake City to Herradura, Puntarenas, Costa Rica were conducted without issue with a cost of about $6,000. Our container arrived within the given time span (about 6 weeks). The owner told us they could not tell what the actual taxes would be until Costa Rican officials review the inventory, but in the end, the amount was less than the quote. All was fine and well until we opened our boxes as movers brought them into our house. I realized the truck driver had contracted help offloading the boxes from the container, but there should have been some sort of responsibility if theft occurred. In the end, my iPhone, a two-thousand dollar Rado watch, a gold coin worth another thousand, my fine jewelry, an mp3 player, and an expensive pocket knife were snatched. The movers stole things out of open boxes and from the rooms they were entering. Charles Zeller promised to purchase and replace our stolen iPhone three different times, but would not replace any of the other goods. In the end, he failed to do anything and stopped answering or returning our calls. My advise to expats would be to make sure the company you choose has insurance that covers damage and theft, read as much about the company and reviews as possible, and lock up all of your valuables in one room you do not grant movers access as they offload your goods. I also wish I would have withheld my final payment to the driver until we had located our most valuable belongings. Do not let the movers rush you.

~ Rona

DOCUMENTATION

No matter which mover you choose, if you request door-door service be prepared to provide: a copy of your passport, and an accurate inventory list (this is how customs calculates your tariffs). After you have arrived in Costa Rica, you will need to provide a copy of the valid entry stamp in your passport.

If you opt to pick up your container at port yourself, make sure and bring an interpreter if you are not fluent in Spanish. Be prepared to pay for stamps at more than one location before you can pay for your tariffs and be awarded your property.

TIP
A good rule of thumb is that most processes involving the Costa Rican government take no less than 3 days to complete. Expect it and experience less headaches when you encounter it.

AVOIDING SCAMMERS

The moving company:

☐ Should not ask for cash deposits before moving your items

☐ Should have a physical address near your area, not a P.O. box

☐ Should be licensed and insured

☐ BBB ratings, American Moving and Storage Association Member (AMSA)

☐ Be wary of low-ball prices

☐ The mover should conduct an in-home evaluation for accurate estimate

ASSOCIATION OF RESIDENTS OF COSTA RICA (ARCR)

If you chose to become a member of ARCR, they will provide information, checklists, and assistance with relocation. Make sure and join the ARCR forums. There is a wealth of information from knowledgeable cedula carrying expats.

www.arcr.net/services/relocate.html

See the end of this chapter for a moving checklist

SHIPPING YOUR CAR

THE MONEY

If your baby is less than 3 years old you will pay 52.29% tax based on the *value* of the car! If your car is 4-5 years old, the tax increases to 63.91%, if it's > 6 years old then it costs your first born child plus 79.03% of it's *value*.

What is the *value* based on you ask? It's based on two pieces of information.

1. What you paid for the car as written on the bill of sale or invoice *plus* the cost required to ship the vehicle to beautiful Costa Rica. For example, Sharon bought her used beetle, Calvin, for $9,000 then she forked out $1,000 bucks to ship it. Her car is *valued* at $10,000.

2. The second resource is the CR equivalent to a Kelly Blue Book. The "Valuation Database of the Ministry of the Treasury" is locally called "Cartica / Autovalor." See web site:
http://www.hacienda.go.cr/autohacienda/AutoValor.aspx
After they have the calculations from both sources, the larger of the two numbers is selected as your *value*!

If Sharon's Beetle was valued at $10,500 by the Cartica and was five years old, the full import tax due would equal:
$10,500 (highest *value*) x .6391 (63.91% for 5 yr. old cars) = $6,710.55 in import taxes

In addition to taxes, Sharon will be forced to pay for stamps, fumigation, and potentially storage fees. There are no less than three lines to wait in at three different locations, not to mention the process to nationalize the car! Is her Beetle worth over $6,700 in taxes, $200-300 in fees, and $1,000 to ship, even if it has a fun name?

Also remember, it's only a matter of time before the CR clay, bumpy roads, and humidity break something. Good luck finding VW parts! They are non-existent in CR. If at all possible, stick with common manufacturers such as: Toyota, Hyundai, and Nissan. When in doubt, observe what model of taxis you see most often.

Also, it's best if you purchase / bring a car with manual transmission. Most mechanics are more versed with MTs since that encompasses the majority of vehicles in CR. The steep hills and clay are too hard on the brakes and can/have led to a malfunction. Brakes are a part of my car that I *DO NOT* want to malfunction!

EXPERIENCE

Brad Butler reported on www.emeraldforestproperties.com the following costs for shipping his little Toyota that he purchased for $1,500:

"Cost of car $1,500.00
Cost of shipping broker $535
Cost to deliver car to San Jose $250.00 (Did not happen)
Cost of stamps, fumigating and storage fee $530.00
Cost to lawyer to nationalize car $3,500 (asked for more in the end)
Cost in payoffs to speed things up $350.00
  6 months later I was legal at the grand total of: $6,665.00
I priced the same car here and it was under $2000.00"
See the website above for Brad's whole experience.

THE PROCESS

The process for shipping your vehicle includes hiring a moving company *(see the **International Moving** section)* to pick up and pack your car into a cargo shipment. Once the shipment is full, and only once it is full, the car begins its long journey to Costa Rica. It is very possible that no one will actually know when the shipment will fill, but you should be provided an educated guess based on anticipated cargo. Once your baby arrives in Costa Rica, it is placed in line at customs where it will remain until it is evaluated and the import taxes are paid.

SELLING YOUR CAR

I sold my 2 year old Nissan Versa to free up extra cash for my move to Costa Rica. I decided get a true CR car, a 1980 Jeep CJ7. Her name is Ginger.

Initially, I wasn't going to purchase a car. I was going to utilize the cheap public transit but, I moved to CR alone and since the buses shut down early, I wanted the independence a car allowed for. I also didn't want to worry about getting stuck somewhere if I didn't catch a bus in time and was in a town with few taxis.

It was very simple to sell my Versa. I went to Carmax and asked for a quote. After about 25 minutes, their technicians had finished a once over of my car and handed me a printed guaranteed offer. I compared it to Kelly Blue Book, Autotrader, and Craigslist equivalents. Sure, I would miss out on a few hundred bucks but selling with Carmax was easy, convenient, and I could decide what day to give up my baby. So, I returned to Carmax the day before my flight to CR, handed the sales team the guaranteed offer (good for one week), and asked to complete the sale. 20 minutes later, I walked out the door with a check!

ELECTRONICS

Decide which electronics you will need in CR and pack them. Keep in mind that house construction uses cement walls, so wifi signals do not reach beyond one- two rooms. My condo consists of two levels. I have a booster (airport express) that I plug in at the top of the stairs. The booster catches the wifi signal from my combo cable modem/wifi router and boosts the signal to the rest of the upper level. Being a bit of a tech geek, I wanted to have access to the internet in my upstairs bedroom in addition to the lower level and my Airport Express accomplishes that goal.

If you are moving to an area serviced by a cable provider, it is a good idea to bring your own cable modem/wifi router. This way you don't have to rent one from the cable company and can bring up-to-date hardware avoiding unnecessary slowing or glitches caused by older electronics. With the humidity in CR, any old electronic is most likely broken or unreliable. Even with a de-humidifier, it is difficult to keep the water-filled air from rusting and destroying gadgets.

If you enjoy reading print books and magazines, it will be more difficult to get your hands on English materials. Without easy ordering from Amazon or driving to your local Barnes N' Nobles, eReaders are the most convenient option. Sure you can't smell the book or see how far you are by gauging the remaining thickness but you can shop in the Nook, Kindle, and iBook store from the hammock in your villa, instantly downloading your next reading pleasure.

OTHER ELECTRONICS:
- Laptop
- iPad
- Up-to-date smartphone *(who knows when you will be able to buy a new one)*
- Mobile speakers
- Apple Tv[14]
- Waterproof case for your phone (for those refreshing downpours on your beach walks)
- External hard drive to back up all of the amazing photos you will take

---

[14] a device that connects to your TV's HDMI input and allows you to sign into your Netflix and Hulu accounts, rent off of iTunes, and access and Apple computer music and video library right on your HD TV

- Power surge protector- you can pick this up in CR but make sure you use it. Lightening strikes have literally blown up appliances here
- *Thumb/Flash drive* to take documents from your computer to be printed at a Copia store
- *Video c*amera and waterproof camera with extra batteries *(what good is a dead camera?)*
- Nice pair of *headphones* with a mic for Skype.
- UPS (Uninterrupted Power Supply) is a devise that is $40-$150 that allows for you to have uninterrupted power (by utilizing battery power) when you loose electricity in a storm. It has plugs and looks like a power surge on one side, and the other side harbors batteries. It stores energy while electricity is there, when the power goes out then you have about 1.5-2 hours of battery time. *(Great for those telecommuters that need to keep the cable modem on)*
- 140W adapter for your car (plug your computer in while on long road trips)

STREAMING MUSIC AND VIDEO

If you are accustomed to Pandora, I have good news and bad news for you. At the time of my writing, they do not have licensing for Costa Rica. The good news is you can download a free program to "bounce" your IP address. In normal person speak that means the program will play hide-and-seek with the numbers that tell the internet where connection is coming from. The program that I have used is called Tor. Open Tor after downloading the free program from www.torproject.org and search for Pandora in Tor's web browser. You can listen to all of the music that you want. Another option for music streaming is Spotify which has no restrictions functioning in Costa Rica.

The sun goes down around 6pm year round in Costa Rica. With extra time on your hands in the evening, movie nights can be a great solution!

Netflix does work in Costa Rica but will not be identical to the Netflix from the States. Since there is no DVD subscription, it offers more instant watch options. While the catalog is larger, they take away some instant watches that you can view for free in the United States. I'm guessing that it relates to the specific movie/show's copyright rules.

Amazon's prime instant watches are growing more and more popular. Unfortunately, they are not licensed in Costa Rica either. The fix is the same as the previously mentioned Pandora. Simply download a free IP bouncer like Tor and search for the movie on Amazon's website through Tor's website browser.

BEST APPS FOR EXPATS

Jump into the app store and be immediately lost, intimidated, and frustrated. How do you find quality apps that will suit you? Mostly, by word of mouth. As an expat who is a former Apple employee and a total mac geek, let me share with you my favorite apps specifically for the expat.

Skype

Probably, the most used and most valuable app for expats. This as a must have app. So you have downloaded Skype on your computer. Once you have a smart phone or tablet, download the free app, and sign in.

I highly recommend making two purchases on Skype, an unlimited calling subscription and a personalized phone number. I purchased the subscription that allowed unlimited calling to landlines and cell phones in the United States. I paid around $3 a month. Rates constantly change with different promos, but typically Skype rewards you for paying for the entire year in advance. The other purchase was just as important. If you don't purchase a number then businesses, family, and friends can't call you. While you can call them anytime you want, they will see a different number each time and not know it's you. You can choose your area code when you purchase a number.

I take Skype with me everywhere I can get cell service on my iPhone. That way I can make a call to loved ones or for business back to the

States. If anyone needs to reach me, and I have Skype logged in on my phone, it will ring!

There are competing apps that offer similar phone service, Vonage, magicJack, and TextPlus. Skype has been at it the longest, has a proven track record and adds video conferencing and instant message features.

TextPlus

In case you have been under a rock for the last 5-7 years, texting is practically required to keep in touch with people. I know some who refuse to answer their phone, but will quickly respond to a text. International text messages get pricy if you don't know about great apps like TextPlus.

Build a free account, choose your number with any area code you'd like and text away! Ask your friends and family to add the number to their address book as text message only so they will know it is you. The old edition required you to use wifi to send/receive messages, but was recently updated so anytime you are connected to the internet (3g or wifi) you can use the app. There is also an option to call from the app but I do not recommend this feature because while it is cheap international calling, Skype wins my money when it comes to calls. *See Skype for more info.*

Voxer

"Breaker Breaker, Ginger's on the move." I loved walkie talkies as a kid. This app allows you to talk to other people just like you are both on walkie talkies except you are not restricted to a 200 foot range. You could walkie talkie with someone in Africa if they have the app and a cellular signal.

If you hate text messaging, you'll love this. If you find that the second you get behind the wheel you need to text everyone talk into the phone instead and they will get your walkie message.

The downside of this app is the other person must also have the app but they don't have to be logged in to receive the message. The app will notify them of a new message waiting to be heard. In order to talk back and forth in real time, both parties need to have the app open.

Google Voice

Google Voice allows the user to transfer their phone number to Google Voice and then forward it to a second number! Currently, they do not allow forward to an international number, but you can forward it to your Skype number! Also, if you are connected to wifi you can use it to make calls and text for free to the States *(if that is where you have it set up)*. To learn more about how Skype and Google Voice can integrate see:

http://lifehacker.com/5878980/how-to-make-skype-play-nicely-with-google-voice

XE Currency

This app is exactly what it sounds like, a currency converter. It's nice to keep an eye on the currency transaction rates so you know what's a good deal. You can also show the small shop owner what the current rate is and bargain if using USD. It may not work, but it's worth a shot. Plus, if you explore in neighboring Nicaragua or elsewhere it's very helpful.

Google Translate

A translator app that every expat should have in their arsenal is Google Translate. Even if you are not in the smart phone arena, make sure and take advantage of Google Translate on your computer. The biggest drawback to the app is that it requires cellular service or wifi to work. If you are struggling with the same word, however, it remember previous translation requests.

Card Reader

For business owners, a mobile device card-reader is a great addition to your financial tools. One card-reader/ merchant account does not fit all. I'll highlight the most popular choices and you can decide which one fits your companies needs the best.

Flagship ROAMpay
- Ranked #1 by Top Ten Reviews
- Geo-tag[15] each transaction
- 0.38-1.58% commission!
- iPhone, iPod Touch, iPad, Android, Blackberry compatible
- 0 monthly & setup fees
- Free card reader

Square
- 2.75% commission
- 0 monthly & set up fees
- Free card reader
- Hardware accessories like Cash Register stand for the iPad

Paypal
- 2.7% commission
- Free card reader
- 0 monthly & set up fees
- Add a Pay with Paypal button to your web site
- Bill me later options (you get paid upfront and the customer can receive your product without paying a nickel for up to 6 months!)

---

[15] Geotagging marks the GPS coordinates of a location

For an excellent review conducted by Top Ten Reviews go to:
http://iphone-card-reader-review.toptenreviews.com

TripIt

As an avid traveler, I love this app! It is the ultimate travel organization app. Sometimes I book my airfare, hotels/ hostels, and rental cars months out while other times only days out. After downloading TripIt, creating an account and authorizing it to access my email, I no longer need to worry about printing or organizing my confirmation emails. I used to search my email for these confirmation codes, reservation codes, etc. Now, TripIt recognizes when I receive an email confirmation that pertains to travel. The app automatically adds it and sends me an email alert that it has the confirmation email.

It also allows you to create trips. I recently returned from a three month trip to South America. I was able to separate all of my reservations by creating multiple trips: Machu Picchu trip, Ecuador trip, and going home trip. Soon thereafter, I added a wedding trip and a honeymoon trip! It was so great to see all of my complex plans organized so clearly without an ounce of effort on my part! Also, when I create a new trip, I can place the date span. After I set the dates, any new confirmations for those dates automatically get added to the corresponding trip! I can access my trip info on my iPad, my iPhone, or any computer at Tripit.com. How great is that?

Airport Ace *(iPhones only)*

This app provides detailed information for most major airports. It provides all parking options and their corresponding fees. It lists food and shopping options for each terminal complete with maps. SJO has not been added yet, but most layovers getting to SJO are included. I primarily use this app to decide where I am going to grab a bit to eat on a quick layover, so I don't loose time searching in the terminal.

Convert Units

This is really only needed if you are from the US. Since the United States is hell bent on being different, we don't know: what price per kilo gets us, if we are speeding at 50 kph, how much space is 1000m^2, or how large is 2 hectares of land. Until you learn these new measurements an app like Convert Units is very helpful.

Kindle

Everyone has heard about the Kindle. What you might not have heard is how hard it is to find books written in English in Costa Rica. Unless you are in San José or other large town, it is near impossible. So, even though I prefer a book in my hand over a screen, I have completely sold out to the Kindle App. It's nice to have all of my books in my skinny iPad and iPhone. I chose the Kindle App over iBooks and the Nook. Kindle, as an Amazon derivative is often $2 or $3 cheaper than the Barnes N' Noble's Nook. All 3 programs have similar interfaces, so no deciding factor there. The Kindle has more book options than any other book app. Surprising, since I am a Mac geek, but I don't see any Apple oohs and aws like I usually do, to use their application in this instance. I miss Steve Jobs...

Dropbox-

Dropbox has been around for awhile now and it still does a great job storing your documents. There are numerous competitors now: CX, Cloudme, TeamDrive, ShareFile Egnyte, Huddle, Cubby, Syncplicity , Box, Amazon Cloud Drive, Wuala, SugarSync, SpiderOak, and Microsoft Live Mesh to name a few. I'm sure that many are just as good as Dropbox. So far, I have stuck with DB because it has never failed and that kind of consistency with my key documents is important to me. They have tried to spruce things up by adding a photo loader that launches anytime a camera is hooked up to your computer, but I don't pay for extra space on DB, therefore, I don't use the photo launcher. A free subscription caps at 2 GB which is plenty for thousands of documents. I have many of my documents and manuscripts backed up for my publishing business on Drop Box. I use an external drive for my video production company, and a second external hard drive to back up my entire computer (pictures and video included).

Don't be caught without a backup in the States or in Costa Rica. You cannot recreate the memories captured by your thousands of pictures. I'm also sure you don't want to re-create that presentation for work or rebuild your music collection. In Costa Rica, your computer liability increases. The humidity is like kryptonite to your hard drive, sand is the devil, and you can be sure that both will be in your computer if you live near the beach.

Facebook

While you may not have been a "Facebooker" in the past, once you live in a different country you may re-think your stance. Facebook provides a way to stay connected and informed in your loved ones' lives. You can see pictures from their trips, watch their children grow up, and comment on each adorable photo, making a virtual appearance in their lives when a physical one is not possible. You can also share with them the adventures you are having in Costa Rica. I know from experience that people love seeing new exotic places. After seeing some of your gorgeous photos, they might be compelled to plan a trip to visit you!

Photocard

The post office system in Costa Rica is flawed at best. Packages arriving empty is not uncommon. Postcards usually make it to the States but take 4-8 weeks! Photocard is a cool app that lets you assign a picture you have taken on your iPhone/ iPad as the postcard cover, then allows you to write a message in a variety of fonts and sizes. It even has stickers so you can decorate the card. Once completed, you purchase one credit for $2.99 to have it printed and put into the US mail that day! With a 2-3 day turnaround, your grandkids, buddies, parents, or clients can have a fun, personal, and customized card from you!

Weatherbug for iPhone

I enjoy the interface of this weather app on the iPhone. It has great radar quality, and you can easily add different cities around the world so you can call up your family and ask them how the snow feels.

KVUE WX for iPad-

This is my favorite interface for the iPad as it is aesthetically very pleasing! It includes: hourly forecast, windchill, heat index, wind speed and direction, sunrise / sunset and a variety of other handy bits of information easily viewed.

SET UP YOUR COMMUNICATION SYSTEM

UNLOCK YOUR PHONE

Almost all phones purchased in North America are locked by their original carrier so that only sim cards provided by the carrier will function with the phone. Make certain that you can unlock the phone for use in Costa Rica. Otherwise, the phone is no good to you as an expat.

The first thing is to determine is if you are in contract with your service provider. If you are in contract, then you will have to either finish your term or pay a steep early cancellation fee. After your contract has expired or terminated, you should be eligible to unlock your phone.

Each carrier handles the unlock differently. AT&T has a customer service department that is "supposed to" unlock your phone after receiving a written request and the phone's IMEI number. I tried this route numerous times for my iPhone with no response. I found that using $10 and a third party service was the way to go. There are numerous services that do an excellent job providing you with a factory unlock (i.e. no hacking) within 24 hours. One that I have used successfully numerous times is:

http://unlimitedtalkdatatext.com/unlock/

T-Mobile's policy is that as long as there is no balance remaining on the purchase of your phone, they will unlock the phone. Simply dial 611 which directs you to their customer service. Tell them you are going on a trip abroad and need the phone unlocked.

If you have another service provider or an android phone visit the website above and use the virtual assistant. Ask if they can unlock your specific phone and they will let you know. If you have a phone with Verizon, Sprint, MetroPCS, Cricket, or U.S. Celluar, then it's time to go shopping because they are CDMA phones and will not work in Costa Rica. Costa Rica is in conjunction with the rest of the world on the GSM network. If this is all Greek to you, pretend that GSM is on one radio station, CDMA is on another, and the dial is broke. The US decided to be different opting for the CDMA network when it was new and exciting. So you can put your old phone next to your yard stick on your way out of the country.

BANDWIDTH

Make sure that your phone supports the bandwidth that the service providers utilize. You can go to www.phonearena.com and enter in your phone to find out which frequencies it supports.

ICE/Kolbi: GSM 1800 – UTMS 850
Claro: GSM 1800 – UTMS 2100
Movistar: GSM 1800 – UTMS 850/2100

SKYPE

Features:

- Skype to Skype Calling
- International Calls
- Call waiting
- Video
- Messaging
- Sharing
- Personalized number
- Smart phone app

If you are not already a Skype user then go to www.skype.com and create a new account. Take care to remember your user name so you can give it to your loved ones. After you create an account, make sure all of the people that you wish to "Skype" with have also created accounts. Try a few trial runs and work out the bumps. Call up your daughter, son, or BFF and ask them to login. Stay on the phone in case they encounter "technical difficulty." Test video conferencing, instant messaging, voice calls, and sending pictures or files over Skype. So when you are thousands of miles away, you will already know how it works and the process required. If you choose Skype as your main source of international communication, then you will want to purchase a personalized phone number and subscription. See the **Communication, After You Have Arrived** section for more information.

TEXT MESSAGING

Texting has become a form of communication to keep in touch with our younger generation. In fact, there is a whole new language being created around texting. BRB... Ok, I'm back!

International texting gets pricey fast! There is a solution with a few excellent apps that allow you to text for free. *I use TextPlus which I covered above in Best Apps For Expats.* Your Skype account will allow you to text but it will cost you. The amount is displayed in the lower right corner of the texting space. It usually ranges from $0.09-.15 cents per message. You have to add "Skype Credit" before you can text.

magicJack
- International Calls
- Call waiting
- Transfer your number
- Use a regular phone!
- Smart Phone app
- Caller ID

The most popular internet phone services are Skype and magicJack hands down. If you prefer to use a wireless phone or even a wired phone at home, magicJack has some extraordinary gizmos so you don't have to take the call through your computer. Skype has come out with RTX DUALphone 4088 ($90 USD) recently to respond to the magicJack Plus. MJ also has free call waiting! You are required to purchase the device that translates the cable-modem signal to a phone jack receiver. You need a regular phone or computer to use the magicJack. You can either transfer your number or select a new one. They provide a 30 day free trial, but you are required to pay a subscription. If you decide to go with the magicJack, make sure and order the device before departure and bring a phone with you so you can take advantage of all the options!

DATA

Many people experience difficulty setting up their data services with their iPhone, iPad, or other smart device using CR service providers. If this sounds familiar, make an adjustment to your APN settings. If you have no idea where the setting is located, Google "Where is the APN setting on a _____ phone?" See the **back of the book** for appropriate APN settings for each CR cellular provider.

MOVING CHECKLIST

☐ go to www.intlmovers.com and get quotes and companies that serve your two points of location

☐ ask for recommendations from friends, expat forums, ARCR, and read testimonials found in this chapter

☐ Double check with the BBB regarding the potential company

☐ Find out what the mover will do if an item is damaged in transit

☐ Obtain at least three estimates from various companies and compare their costs with their corresponding services and ratings.

☐ Find out if the mover is registered with FMCSA. http://ai.fmcsa.dot.gov/hhg/Search.asp?ads=a

☐ Determine when and how your items will be picked up

☐ Acquire all contact information for the movers for each step of the process: before, during, and after the move

☐ Purchase insurance for your items

Moving Day

☐ If at all possible, be present to answer questions and oversee work

☐ Make sure to watch the inventory process and make sure the condition of your items is correctly documented because this list is used to calculate your taxes

☐ Keep your bill until you have all possessions in your new home and all claims are settled if applicable

☐ After the truck drives away perform a final walk through so you don't forget anything

☐ Make sure that the appropriate party has directions to your new home in Pura Vida!

☐ Update your contact information, if it changes, when you arrive in Costa Rica with the movers and drivers

Delivery Day

☐ Be present to answer any questions, inventory the boxes, and direct traffic.

☐ Supervise unloading, unpacking (if applicable) of your goods.

☐ Make sure that the inventory list reflects any damaged items before you sign any documents

☐ Pay your driver, or sign documents authorizing payment, according to the terms of your agreement.

After You Arrive

You have arrived after you step off the plane, through the humid jetway, and out the doors where the warm moist air greets you to Costa Rican soil.

Bienvenido a Costa Rica
"Welcome to Costa Rica"

Welcome to your new life as an expat. Make sure to take in this moment, celebrate it! Don't rush past it, you are no longer in a hurry. Settle into the rhythm of the country.

If you were unable to make an exploratory trip to explore the regions and secure housing, make sure to plan for at least a few weeks of exploration, hotel/hostel stay while you find your rental. The last thing you want to do is jump into the first rental you see since the region and your home will greatly affect your overall satisfaction with life in

Costa Rica. The more places you tour, the better suited the selected home will be.

COLONES

While the US dollar is accepted in many large towns and tourist hubs, your change will be colorful plastic bills and heavy coins. As an expat, I try to avoid using US currency because I want to embrace and support the Costa Rican Colon. That being said, if you work in the tourism industry or other industry that sees a lot of US dollars, then it will be a part of your regular currency experience.

Let me teach you a basic conversion you can use to ballpark the cost of an item (if you are accustomed to the US dollar). The transaction rate hovers around ₡500 colones for $1 USD. With totals in the thousands of colones, it can get confusing. The trick is two-fold. Take away the last three zeros and double the number you are left with. Take a check of 21,000 colones. After taking away the last 3 zeros, you have 21. Now double it, and you have 42. The check is in the neighborhood of $42 USD. The gorgeous green bills have 10,000 on them. How much does it convert to in USD?

FINDING A RENTAL

North Americans and Europeans are planners. We want to know exactly where we are going, how long we will be there, and exactly how much "there" will cost. This way of living does not completely jive with the culture of Costa Rica. While it is possible to arrange where you will be staying ahead of time and sign a lease for a year before you arrive, I highly discourage it. If you do not want to spend the beginning of your trip looking at houses and regions then I suggest you take a separate "scouting" trip some time before the actual move. A trip dedicated to viewing houses and condos for rent and exploring the area is a necessity! See how far away the grocery store is, where the bus station or gas stations are located. After you have viewed at least 8-10 homes, write down a list of must haves and wants, to see which home suits you best. Judge the residence with the W-A-S-P-S acronym discussed in the *Where in Costa Rica is Your Paradise* section.

PURCHASING A HOME

If you haven't yet, read the ***Try Before You Pry*** section before you proceed.

The first step is to gather referrals for an excellent attorney making sure the referrals are from people who actually purchased property through him/her. Then set up an appointment and ask any and all questions you have about purchasing property after you have read this guide.

Next, start searching for properties in your desired location. If you opt to have an agent assist you, know that there are no real estate regulations in place in Costa Rica. That means, someone could literally be an agent with zero knowledge of the market. It also means their commission is not regulated. I would recommend going with an agent who has multiple positive referrals from expats who have made purchases through him/her. You need to ask what their commission is upfront, and if it ever changes for any circumstances. Get the answers in writing!

There is no such thing as an exclusive agent, so feel free to shop around and see which agent you like the best, and who shows you properties that are closer to your wish list and budget.

Once you have located a property or home to purchase, had your attorney review the title and give you the ok, you or your agent will present the buyer with a written offer and an earnest money deposit.

Maritime Zone
Law No. 6043 (March 2nd, 1977)

Every beach is a beach for the people in Costa Rica. There is no such thing as a private beach, even if you have a beachfront home. The first 200 meters measured from the high tide line represents the Maritime Zone. Inside the Maritime Zone is the Public Area which is measured as the first 50 meters from the high tide line. The Public Area is just that, meant for the public and cannot be purchased. Costa Ricans have a right to enjoy any coastal area they desire.

Beachfront properties have *fee simple titled* which provides the same conditions of ownership to foreigners as it does to Costa Ricans.

A Fee Simple Title is a type of ownership used in common law countries. It entitles the owner to use or sell the property at their will with the large caveat that the government has eminent domain. Therefore, if they decided there should be a park constructed where your property lies in the Maritime Zone then you can pack your bags.

If you decide to move forward with a Maritime Zone land purchase, take care in dotting your I's and crossing your T's. The government is very strict about permits, especially pertaining to Maritime Zones. They require specific permissions from the Instituto Castarricense de Turismo . If everything checks out, then and only then, can you proceed WITH your lawyer to make the purchase.

You can ask for a specified amount of time before closing similar to an escrow period in the States. If you and the seller agree to a period of time, you enter into a Opció de Compra *(option to buy),* or a Promesa Recíproca de Compraventa *(Reciprocal Promise to Buy and Sell).* The actual transfer of funds would not occur until closing when the transfer of the deed or Escritura de Traspaso occurs in front of a notary public.

Notary publics in Costa Rica do a lot more than apply their stamp. They have to be attorneys and are granted extensive powers from the state. After the transaction occurs, the notary or attorney registers the sale at the National Registry in San José.

CORPORATIONS, S.A.

Many expats opt to purchase their home and vehicles in the name of a Corporation *(Sociedad Anónima, S.A.)* that they create which limits their liability within Costa Rica. Costa Rican courts do not make a habit of seeking funds through the Corporation for debts owed by an individual. Therefore, if you as an individual have financial problems or claims against you, property owned through an S.A. would not be affected.

In Costa Rica, if you are involved in an at fault collision with a Tico that is critically injured, a claim against you may be filed. It is not nearly as litigious as the States, but having an extra layer of security on your property, house, or car is helpful through the creation of an S.A.

When it comes time to sell, you can simply sell the stock of the S.A which decreases closing costs. No transfer of title is necessary because the title is in the Corporation, or S.A. There is an annual fee to maintain the Corporation.

AFECTACIÓN FAMILIAR/ HOMESTEAD

One option for married couples is to purchase the home as an Afectación Familiar (homestead). The benefit here is the property cannot be mortgaged, both parties have equal ownership to the property, and the house is shielded by creditors of either spouse. Only the joint debts of the couple can be filed against the property.

REAL ESTATE AGENTS: *Use with Caution*

There is no regulation in CR regarding Real Estate Agents, therefore, they can charge anything they want on top of the purchase price if you are not mindful. Which is why we recommend you ask from the start what their fee is and get it in writing! Find out how many people are getting to partake of this purchase. Is the real estate's friend who referred you getting a cut, the taxi driver who drove you to the appointment, the dog who saw you approaching the building and looked extra cute to draw you in? See if they are getting additional money from you on top of the agents fees. To read more about the escrow process and fees read the *Purchasing a Home* section.

SQUATTERS

The last thing that any homeowner wants is squatters in their house. In the United States, it's a health, safety, and financial hazard. In Costa Rica, you are in danger of loosing your property. *Listen up part-time expats!* Squatters have rights in CR, land ownership functions differently in CR. You need to be aware of these rights when stepping into ownership in CR.

In the late 1800s, laws were enacted that allowed free poor farmers to settle on unused land. To this day, CR wants every Tico to have his cut of land. One of the goals of these laws was to prevent the upper class from owning all of the land.

If squatters occupy your "unoccupied" house and land and work for three months on the property, they start to accrue property rights. After only a year, they can apply for its expropriation from the "absentee landlord."

What do you do if you find out a squatter is on your property? You must immediately file for an eviction order. If it is within the first three months and you can prove that, the procedure is simple enough. If you drag your feet or don't learn about the squatters until it is too late then the process becomes long, drawn out, and exhausting.

When purchasing a house, take extra care to make sure signs of squatters are not present. If there is a caretaker of the property make sure that they really are a caretaker and not a squatter that may already have rights to the same property you seek to purchase. If you are concerned about squatters, film your property frequently so you have proof of improvements and changes demonstrating the property is not abandoned.

If you plan to be gone for an extended period, make sure you have a caretaker on the property to keep out squatters. You can put an ad in the "Caretaker Gazette" for someone to house/pet sit your property. You provide the chores to be completed daily and the time span they will reside on your property. In exchange for taking care of your property, they receive a free place to live! It's a win win! Create a written contract that each party signs so that he/she cannot become a squatter. In addition, have a neighbor or close friend that you trust keep an eye on the property, popping in to say hi, and check out the place every few months.

SETTING UP UTILITIES

If you have rented your home, utilities are more than likely already set up for you. Don't expect them to be changed into your name. It is so difficult to change the account that most landlords don't even bother. Make sure that if the utilities are not included in your rent, you are given the account numbers, and corresponding account owners names for the water and electric bills. That comes in handy when it's time to pay!

With the account information in hand, you can pay your electric bill at any I.C.E. building or better yet at most large grocery stores (the line is much smaller). Simply supply them with your electric bill account number. They usually will retort with the name on the account. You verify it is correct and pay the amount owed. You are then given a receipt. www.ice.go.cr

To pay your water bill, you must locate the nearest National Institute of Aqueducts and Sewage location. www.aya.go.cr

Your internet provider is the only utility that is often placed in your name unless your landlord includes it in your rent. If there is a cable provider in your area, you will be required to schedule an appointment (*providers include: CableTica, ICE DSL, Amnet, and RACSA*) to come out and show you the plans they offer, sign a contract and turn on service. Afterwards, you have a choice of paying your bill at their office or set up automatic payments.   When I signed up, I was given the first 3 months free. I would not recommend signing up for the automatic payments since their system has flaws yet to be worked out. Two different months my service was turned off for "failure to pay." After calling and asking why the internet was turned off, I told them that was incorrect and that I was enrolled in their automatic payment plan. They looked it up and saw I had indeed paid and reactivated my service.

In addition to having my service wrongly shut off twice, they also continued to charge my card for 4 months after I had cancelled their service. I called them numerous times and after five or six attempts, finally reached someone who confirmed they were indeed charging me in error. They remembered my email about canceling service but couldn't find it. This is just one of many frustrating experiences in Costa Rica and you have to just roll with it. I finally got my refund but only when I disputed the charges with my credit card company.

LOCAL COMMUNICATION

LANDLINE

Obtaining a landline connection in Costa Rica is for those strong of heart. If your house has a pre-existing landline then you struck fixed line gold! It seems like it takes an act of god to set up a new landline. First, landlines are only for residents. Second, there are a limited number of available phone lines for new customers. You could be on a waiting list for weeks, months, or even years!

If you wish to be placed on a list for a fixed line, you need to provide your name, service address, passport number, the electricity meter number, and the phone number of the nearest fixed line. Once your turn finally arrives, you will need to drop around $100 USD for installation. If you are lucky and have an existing but unactivated line, $30 USD will get you rolling.

If you have an active fixed line, you can pay the monthly bill at an I.C.E. office or online.

CELL PHONE

If you have a CDMA phone (Verizon, Sprint, UScell, or Cricket) it is no good in CR. It's best if you purchase your GSM phone[16] in the US because phones are expensive and difficult to come by in CR. Do not forget to assure that it is unlocked and not under contract with a provider! *See more about unlocking your phone in the Before You Leave section.*

Take your passport, your unlocked GSM phone, and about 5,000 colones ($10 USD) to either I.C.E., Movistar, or Kolbi. Purchase a new prepaid sim card, or *prepago,* and put the rest of the money on the account so you have some minutes available for use. Drop the sim card in your phone and you will be wireless! Ask around and find out which service provider has the best coverage in your area.

If your town does not have internet providers, or you wish to have internet on the go with your laptop or other electronic device, you can purchase a 3G stick with one of the previously mentioned cellular providers.

---

[16] GSM phones in laymen's terms are the phones that use sim cards

INTERNATIONAL COMMUNICATION

Hopefully you have already set up your Skype account (or other provider mentioned), subscribed to the best unlimited calling plan for your situation, and purchased a unique phone number where business connections and loved ones can reach you. If not, read **Communication Set Up** *section* in the *Before You Arrive section.*

If you have a smart phone, launch Skype and make a test call in that app. Make sure you are dialing from the Skype app otherwise you will be using airtime and long distance fees will apply!

Confirm that everyone you want to contact has Skype accounts and know how to log in. For the technologically challenged, I highly recommend you set up their Skype with them so that you can test out the connection. To add someone to your Skype contacts, click "Contacts" at the top of your screen, then "Add Contact" then key in either their Skype name if you have it, or the email that they used to set up the account. This procedure needs to occur on both sides before you can see both of you are logged into Skype.

Download and install TextPlus on your smart phone as mentioned in the *Before You Arrive section.* Send a trial text message to a loved one and have them send one back. You are up and running!

Make sure and enjoy using FaceTime with others that have Apple products. You can either connect by using their cell phone number or their Apple ID email address. Each route is free utilizing wifi for the connection.

TRANSPORTATION

PURCHASING A CAR

Review **Shipping or Selling Your Car** in the *Before You Arrive* Section to see what models, and specs you should buy in Costa Rica.

Buying a car in Costa Rica is a bit different than purchasing one in North America. One major difference is you use an attorney! The attorney performs a legal search on the placa (license plate) of the car to assure it's not stolen, the title is valid, and their are no open claims against the car. Traffic violations and collision claims are attached to the placa in CR, not your ID. Citizens were able to research this information themselves but a recent change to the system will no longer allow anyone other than an attorney to search *placas.*

After each transaction or sale of a vehicle, papers are filed in the court system because the ownership of the vehicle is regulated by the government. A simple vehicle title cannot guarantee you are the lawful owner until a person designated by the state, (i.e. an attorney), reviews the materials and confirms they are legit.

Shopping for your vehicle can be done on a few different platforms. Craigslist is always a great option, but is not as popular in CR as it is in the US. An even better website for purchasing used cars in CR is www.crautos.com. Also, there are numerous dealerships in Grecia, CR. This region is known as the mecca for car parts and sales.

Ginger was advertised on Craigslist by an expat, so I rode the bus three and a half hours to the Central Valley to take a look. After test driving the car, I decided to purchase. The seller, Paul Roy, and I sat down with a local attorney. I paid Paul with a combination of cash and Paypal, some signatures were scribbled, stamps were smashed, and I went on my merry way in my new old Jeep!

TAXIS

In large towns, taxis are plentiful and affordable only costing a few bucks to drive around town. Long distance trips, on the other hand, can add up. Depending on the time of day, and how much business the driver has received through the day, a 2 hour drive may run you

$125-140 bucks! A shuttle or renting a car for the day is usually a better bet for long distance trip.

RECEIVING YOUR SHIPPED CAR

Receiving your car requires one part resilience, 10 parts patience, and 2 parts cold hard cash! If your command of the Spanish language is not yet up to par, make sure and bring a translator with you.

In order to pay your import taxes and tariffs, you must take your papers to customs to get stamped and pay a fee. Then bring the papers back to the warehouse where your car is stored and be prepared to pay for stamps, fumigating, and storage in addition to your taxes and tariffs. Bring enough cash to pay double the estimated cost so you have a cushion and enough money left over to fuel up. It will have less than $1/8^{th}$ a tank of fuel *(the requested amount to submit your car for transfer)*.

BUS

Learn the bus schedule applicable to your area. The link below contains the schedule throughout the country. If you wish to carry a printed schedule, you can pick one up at any bus station and most tourist centers. Buses are very inexpensive, averaging $1 per hour of drive time. Make sure you keep change in hand for the driver on local buses. For longer trips, purchase your ticket in the bollería at the bus terminal. These long distance buses are often sold with seating assignments so pay attention to the ticket. If it says *asiento* followed by a number, that is your seat assignment.

Make sure to arrive to the parrada, (bus stop), 15 minutes early because buses are often ahead of schedule in CR.
http://www.visitcostarica.com/ict/paginas/LEYES/pdf/ItinerarioBuses_en.pdf

GATHER YOUR BEARINGS

The most frustrating part about moving for me was I had no idea where to get anything. For example, I needed an extension chord, an aux cable, and an adapter to go from the old stereo in my condo to an aux cable input. I hadn't the faintest clue where to find any of these items. In San Diego, I would simply Google Map the nearest Target and be on my way. Not so much in Costa Rica. Not only are there no Home Depots, but even if there was an obvious retail outlet for my wanted item, there would be no online venue to search the location of the nearest store. This is why your landlord, expat community, and Tico friends are very valuable. They have hunted down many of the items that you will need. If they haven't looked for it themselves, their buddy has and found it. Your network is gold! They will help answer:

Where is the grocery store?
Where is the gas station?
Where is a good mechanic? (referral)
Where can you buy hardware items?
Where can you buy furniture?
How do I find a handyman?
Where do I pay my water bill?
Where can I recharge my cell phone?
When in doubt, roll with the flow, wait and then wait some more.

EXPERIENCE

I was visiting Costa Rica for the first time and had a place to stay in Playa Bejuco. I boarded the bus from the Coca Cola station in San José (still named after the Coke plant long destroyed) and I was off to Bejuco, or so I thought. What I neglected to learn was if I was headed to the correct Playa Bejuco. You see, there are two different towns in two different provinces very far apart. One is in Guanacaste in a tiny town with no services. The other is located in Puntarenas just 30 minutes south of Jaco. The distance between the two I would soon find out was about 6 hours.

After I arrived at the first Bejuco, the driver, who only spoke Spanish, was trying to tell me that this was the end of the line. I looked outside to a dark empty piece of land and was puzzled. I called my friend whom I was staying with and she said that she was out on the road and I was in fact not in Bejuco. This went back and forth a few times before the driver offered to talk to my friend who spoke more Spanish that I did. They discovered that I was on the Nicoya Peninsula far away from my actual destination. This worried me because she translated that there were no hotels, and no buses leaving town until 4am! I was stuck!

A few Ticos lingered by the bus understanding that I was in a bind. After they heard what had happened, one kind lady took me by the hand and walked me to her house. She fed me and offered me her bed. I was exhausted but able to rest until 4am when she walked me back to the bus station and made sure that I had the right route to the other Bejuco. God love Ticos!

~ Athena, San Franscico

RECEIVING / ACQUIRING YOUR STUFF

CONTAINER

If you shipped your houseful of belongings, you are in for an excellent lesson in patience. Keep up to date with your shipping company so you will know where your belongings are at all times. Once the company reports that your items are in CR, contact the port and verify the arrival of your container. If you have paid for door-to-door delivery, you will not have to fuss over import duties, tariffs, and loads of paperwork.

Caldera Port:
www.spcaldera.com
Telephone: +506-634-4169

Limón Port:
www.japdeva.go.cr
Telephone: +506-795-4747
Address: PO Box 1320-7300
Puerto Limón, Costa Rica

Expect to pay an import tax based on *their* valuation of your goods. Costa Rica is a member of the World Trade Organization and utilizes the Harmonized System Code (HS Code) for calculating and cataloging imported goods.

FILLING YOUR HOUSE

If you are starting from scratch, there is an excellent chance that the place you are renting/purchasing was already furnished. Many rentals are fully furnished including cutlery and linens. If that is not the case, then ask your real estate agent, neighbors, or expat friends where to buy or have furniture made for you. It is very cheap and fun to have custom woodwork created for your new abode!

EPA is a chain of large Home Depot-like stores where you can find a variety of home necessities to get you started.

Gollo is an appliance and electronics store filled with washer, dryers, TVs, stereos, bikes, blenders, and a few cell phones.

FILING FOR RESIDENCY

Paul Ford worked with the ARCR in order to obtain his cedula. He describes his process:

"After I obtained all the properly notarized documents from the US for my pensionado, I met with the ARCR attorney and filed the paperwork. He took me to get a photograph (they have an irregular passport size), to the police station to get fingerprinted, and then walked me to the immigration office once I was approved. The whole process took about 8 months."

Performing this task on your own is possible as long as you anticipate multiple trips to accomplish one goal.

Some people, like Paul, had very simple processes. Other people, like Jessica and Chris and their four children, did not. They obtained all of the necessary documents for rentista, worked with ARCR, just like Paul did, but were not granted the green light until after 1.5 years!

It took a lawsuit filed by their ARCR lawyer against the immigration department of Costa Rica, before they got their paperwork processed. Their attorney told them that if the immigration office did not respond to the suit within 3 days they would be granted their cedulas. Their first ARCR attorney was fired for misinformation and poor performance.

EXPERIENCE

"We qualified when we originally arrived in 2004 and had the money. We even deposited it in a local bank. Our lawyer swore we needed to leave it in the account for 5 years. "What sense did that make?" we asked. He even called a "friend" who verified this. We had already given him $3,000 for the work. He was absolutely wrong. This was supposed to be one of the "best" law firms in San José. They represent high profile cases. We wanted to use our money, so we opted to wait for my husband's Social Security to begin in a couple of years and re-apply as pensionado. We had our tickets to fly to the States to do all the required paperwork when my husband died. Not being old enough to receive Social Security myself, I waited until my VA benefits were approved. I consulted ARCR and a lawyer in my town who supposedly specialized in immigration and they both gave wrong information regarding whether or not my VA benefits qualified for pensionado. I finally turned to Javier Zavelata with Residency in Costa Rica (www.residencyincostarica.com) and they got me my cedula in 6 months, after an exhausting 5 year battle."

~ Sandra Brooks, Expat Consultant
smbapr@yahoo.com

ESTATE PLANNING

Having your affairs in order is important no matter where you live. When you add the extra complication of an international residency, you need to take extra care in your arrangements for the unfortunate possibility of personal or spousal demise. Death is scary, horrible, and inconceivable... But it's inevitable so we need to plan for it. We don't want to leave our grieving loved ones in a bind. That's the last thing anyone wants.

Consult an attorney from your home country to see how to organize your will to assure that your international residency won't complicate matters. If you purchase property, cars, or maintain a Costa Rican bank account after arriving in CR you should take your US will to a Tico estate planner and create a CR will.

Compare the tax advantages and disadvantages with having a will filed in either country. It very well might make more sense to make your last will in Costa Rica to avoid a hefty inheritance tax that exists in some States. Also, if you own property in CR, it is essential that you file a CR will. Double check with your CPA / attorney that specializes in estate planning.

Take care to include your burial or cremation wishes. This decision is extremely personal, and in some circumstances religious. I will warn you though that flying a body to your home country will cost you a fortune if you're not insured or your insurance does not include repatriation. Plus it is a logistical nightmare with the humidity and heat of Costa Rica. If at all possible, opt to be buried in CR or cremated.

EXPERIENCE

"The laws for death and dying are completely different in countries that are community property States. The uninformed are in for a rude awakening. Costa Rica is a *community property* state. The children, and those who have an inheritance right factor in when one of the spouses dies. We had asked our attorney about creating a will when we bought our property. He promised to get back to us. Never did. I asked him again when Richard was in the hospital. The lawyer had time to go to lunch with people we had referred to him but not to answer my time sensitive questions.

Lesson: Find an attorney that doesn't make excuses but gets the job done without having to ask a second time.

Richard died in the hospital so the OIJ (a form of police) did not have to be involved. In other instances, the body is first taken to check for foul play, and later released. Years ago, we had decided on cremation. Since his death was sudden we had an optional autopsy done. Good move, since the autopsy helped establish that his cause of death was connected to his Vietnam service. (Besides the high profile Agent Orange other things qualify such as asbestosis. Anyone who served during war-time should really research what hazards they were exposed to even if it was 40 years ago.)

The cremation cost approximately $1,700. (I understand plots are a similar expense. You can also rent a plot for 5 years and then have to shop for one to purchase later. No thanks). They provided a nice urn and wooden box I have here. They divided out some ashes for me to take back to the States to give to Richard's children. It's important to have "repatriation of remains" included in a health insurance policy. Morgan White paid for my flight back to the States. They would have paid for the process or returning the body to the US should I have opted for that. We had a funeral service performed by a missionary friend at a local Kingdom Hall of Jehovah's Witnesses so there were no funeral expenses. We also had second service for friends and family in the States."

~ Sandra Brooks, Expat Consultant
smbapr@yahoo.com

TIP

Have a Costa Rican Will!

"If you own things in Costa Rica you must have a CR will! You need to have legal documents in the language of the country, and under the jurisdiction of the local courts. Our property was in the name of a corporation. Those corporate shares needed to be signed by the person who died, otherwise, it is a huge expense. The car was in Richard's name. We had to have it appraised by the court, which cost about $250. I sold one car through the will by 'inheriting' it to a friend, and the other I passed into a corporation that we already owned. I had to have the control of the corporations passed to me as the sole authority. In order to accomplish this I had to gather five friends, two of which, had to be bilingual. Together we performed an extensive process that resulted in transferring the corporation into my name as sole authority. Having a good lawyer was critical! I now have a CR will determining what happens to my corporations.

If you own property and do not have a will your beneficiaries / heirs are required to pay 10% of the value of said house in legal fees to transfer the property into their name. This must be done with the approval of any children that the deceased procreated. The sons and daughters must bring their passports and travel to CR for the process."

~ Sandra Brooks, Expat Consultant
smbapr@yahoo.com

PART III CHECK LIST

- ☐ Make a budget to kill your debts.
- ☐ Assess your current bank and credit cards for international compatibility. Make changes as applicable.
- ☐ Obtain or renew passport(s)
- ☐ Renew drivers license if applicable
- ☐ Gather immigration documents (see immigration section)
- ☐ Decide what to do with your stuff
- ☐ If shipping a container, request at least three estimates from reputable movers
- ☐ Decide which electronics you want to take with you and purchase the electronics that you need for the move
- ☐ If you are a smart phone or tablet kinda' gal/guy, download and play with the best apps for expats
- ☐ Make sure you have an unlocked GSM phone
- ☐ Create a Skype account and share it with loved ones and business colleagues.
- ☐ Download a free text messaging app and try it out. Give your contacts your new texting number before you leave
- ☐ Decide what to do about your car
- ☐ If you are selling your car, prep it, advertise and sell *(Carmax is a great option I have used twice)*
- ☐ If you are shipping your car, get at least three quotes and commit to one

PART IV
FAMILY & EDUCATION

MOVING ABROAD WITH KIDS. DOES IT HINDER OR HARM THEIR FUTURE?
HOW ARE THE SCHOOLS? RAISING KIDS IN COSTA RICA

MOVING WITH A FAMILY

MOVING ABROAD WITH KIDS, DOES IT HINDER OR HARM THEIR FUTURE

Uprooting your family in the pursuit of something better is a scary prospective. Americans have been trained from a very young age that the United States is the best and most sought after country in the world. The truth is the best is not the same from one family to another. One country does not fit all. Costa Rica is no exception.

I'm compelled to remind you there is nothing new about seeking social and economic opportunities elsewhere. Humans are migratory beings, long before the westward movement, people regularly migrated to richer pastures in order to increase their quality of life and, in some cases, to survive. I am a strong proponent of thriving not surviving.

With big business encroaching on middle America, education at a record low, healthcare costs seeming endless, poverty and unemployment at record highs, and quality of life on the decline many people have decided, that now is the time for them to look elsewhere.

Below are a few important questions commonly asked by parents considering migration:

How are the schools? Would I be helping or hindering my children's growth and opportunities? Would we be able to return if we decided it was best for the kids? Is it safe? What is the cost of school?

Moving your family from your place of residence is an extremely personal decision. My goal is to fully inform and answer any questions you have so you can make the best decision for your family. Remember, no decision is a decision in itself. Now, let's address these common concerns.

EDUCATION IN CR

Since 1948, Costa Rica has taken the money that was previously allocated for the military and placed it into education and healthcare. That resulted in an explosion in literacy! Costa Rica's 94.9% literacy earns them one of the highest rates in the world and the number one rank in all of Latin America. The 2012-13 Global Competitiveness Report ranks Costa Rica's overall education 21st out of 133 countries! That is 7 slots HIGHER than the US rank.

The schools in Costa Rica are similar to the United States as in the quality of education ranges greatly from school to school. Schools in the poorest neighborhoods are often less equipped than schools in more affluent regions, just like in the US. The student graduates from public secondary schools after completing the 11th grade.

Costa Rica is home to the world renowned University of Peace to include extra bragging rights!

The most important criteria for most expat parents is accreditation. They want their children to have as many options and open doors as possible.

There are three different degrees that a child can earn while attending school in Costa Rica:

☐ The Costa Rican Bachillerato Diploma which makes you eligible to apply for college in Costa Rica.

☐ The International Baccalaureate Diploma, accredited by the International Baccalaureate Organization in Geneva Switzerland is the most flexible option. This degree makes you eligible to apply for college in the USA, Europe, and Latin America.

☐ The USA High School Diploma which is available at every American private school. This diploma enables you to apply to colleges in the USA, Europe, and many other countries excluding Costa Rica.

Expats have the same three options for schooling that their peers have in their hometown: homeschool, private school, and public school

Oftentimes, foreigners choose to place their children in private bi-lingual schools so their child becomes bi-lingual and acclimates quicker, attending classes taught in both English and Spanish. Others opt for English only schools, hoping not to rock the boat.

HOMESCHOOLING

Homeschooling has gained popularity both in the States and abroad. The only difference is really where "home" is, plus you would be restricted in group and recreational activities designed for groups that are US based. One example of an applicable home based program is Global Village School.

Global Village School

This academy was founded in 1999 by a diverse group of professionals. The academy is

"Internationally accredited, customizable K-12 homeschool diploma program via online and text-based curriculum alongside individualized

teacher services... with an emphasis on peace, justice, diversity, and sustainability." www.globalvillageschool.org

Cost	$USD P/Sem	$USD P/Yr.
K-3	$975	$1,375
4-6	$1,125	$1,575
7-8	$1,275	$1,775

9-12 fee structures *per class*

One-quarter Course (9 weeks): $325 p/course

Semester Courses (5 months)

$525 p/course

Year-long Courses (10 months)

$795 p/course

High School Enrollment fee: $625

Curriculum/Books: $30-60 p/class

For a thorough curriculum review see:
http://blog.denschool.com/educating-the-whole-child-a-global-village-school-curriculum-review/

K-12.com

This site allows you to navigate international education from a variety of school options ranging from public to preparatory. If you maintain an address in the US and pay taxes in that state, *(maybe a family member's address for your mail)*, you can select the corresponding state and enroll in online public school. Go to www.k-12.com to learn more.

PRIVATE SCHOOLS

There are hundreds of private and Catholic school options and just as many price-tags. In the past, the quality schools were located in the Central Valley where the majority of residents live. Due to the influx of expats from America, Europe, and Canada, quality private schools are slowly popping up across the coast, but the hub is certainly still in the valley.

Below is a list of private schools in alphabetical order.

American International School of Costa Rica

Pre-K - 12th / Cariari & Heredia
www.aiscr.org
ais@aiscr.org
Telephone: +506-2293-2567
Fees:
$750 matriculation
$4,850- 8,900 annual tuition
$1,000-1,700 annual bus
$1,800-3,800 special programs (ESL/LSP)

Arandu Elementary School

Pre-K - 6th / Escazú
www.arandu.co.cr
aranduk@racsa.co.cr
Telephone: +506-2288-6113
Fees:
$664 enrollment
$664 tuition p/mo
Additional unknown fees for: textbooks, school supplies, & student insurance

Blue Valley School

Pre-K - 12 / Escazú

www.bluevalley.ed.cr
bvschool@racsa.co.cr
Telephone: +506-2215-2203
Fees:
$1,500 one time enrollment
$577- $872 p/mo based on grade

British School

Pre-k - 12 / San José
www.thebritishschoolofcostarica.com
britsch@racsa.co.cr
Fees:
$1,189 one time enrollment
$632-$905 tuition
$100+ bus annually

Cloud Forest School

K-11 / Monteverde
www.cloudforestschool.org
info@cloudforestschool.org
Telephone: +506-2645-5161
Fees:
$6,000-8,500 annual tuition
Tuition includes: bus, Spanish as a Second Language with private or small group instruction 5x/week, wifi use on campus, and a liaison.

Colegio Santa Margarita

7-11 / San Antonio de Belen
www.colegio.santamargarita.ed.cr
admin@santamargarita.ed.cr
Telephone: +506-2239-6293
Fees: Unknown

Colina Azul School

Pre-K - 6 / Atenas

www.atenasprivateschool.com

colinaazual@gmail.com

Telephone: +506-2446-4027

Fees: Unknown

Country Day School

Pre-k -12 / Escazú
www.cds.ed.cr
cdsadmin@cds.ed.cr
Telephone: +506-2289-0919
$1,000 one time enrollment
$700 - $1,050 matriculation
$4,600 - $12,920 annual tuition

Country Day School Guanacaste

Pre-k - 12 / Brasilito
www.cdsgte.com
info@cds.ed.cr
Telephone: +506-2654-5044
Fees:
$1000 one time enrollment
$750 Matriculation each year
$3,150 - $10,500 annual tuition
$1,134 - $1,233 annual bus fees

European School

Pre-K - 12 / Heredia
www.europeanschool.com
info@europeanschool.com
Telephone: +506-2261-0717
Fees:
$500 registration per year
$5380 - $9,180 annual tuition
Tuition includes lunch, books, and notebooks.

Falcan International School- *closing*

Green Life Academy

Pre-K - 12 / Playas del Coco
http://greenlifeacademycr.com
info@mygreenlifeacademycr.com
Telephone: +506 2670-0161
Fees: unknown

Green Valley School

Pre-K - 11 / Vista Atenas
www.greenvalleyatenas.com
greenvatenas@racsa.co.cr
Telephone: +506-2446-8281
Fees: Unknown

Humboldt School (German)

Pre-K - 12 / San José
Spanish/ German school
www.humboldt.ed.cr
Telephone: +506-2232-1455
Fees:
$595 matriculation
$5,906 annual tuition

ILPPAL

9-12 / Santa Ana
No Website but they do have a FB page:
https://www.facebook.com/ColegioILPPAL
ilppal@ice.co.cr
Fees: unknown

International Christian School

Pre-K - 12 / Heredia or Liberia
www.icscostarica.org
avillalobos@icscostarica.org
Telephone: +506-2241-1445
Fees: unknown

Las Nubes

K-11 / Herradura
www.lasnubes.ed.cr
osolano@lasnubes.ed.cr
Telephone: +506-2643-6128
Fees: Approximately $800 in books, uniforms and yearly fees
$320 p/mo tuition

Lincoln School

Pre-K - 12 / San Miguel
www.lincoln.ed.cr
director@lincoln.ed.cr
Telephone: +506-2247-6600
Fees: difficult to discern, see link
http://www.edline.net/pages/LincolnCostaRica/Admissions/
Requirements

Marian Baker

Pre-K-12 /San Ramon de Tres Rios
www.mbs.ed.cr
Director@marianbakerschool.com
Telephone: +506-2273-3426
Fees:
$200 application fee
$1,200 facility development fee
$1,100 registration fee
$5,935 - $11,910 annual tuition
Tuition includes: textbooks, workbooks, computer lab usage, school materials, vision & hearing exam, yearbook, and accidental insurance.

Monteverde Friends School

K-12 / Monteverde
www.mfschool.org
mfschool@racsa.co.cr
Telephone: +506-2645-5302
Fees:

$30 application fee
$150 registration fee
$200-640 p/mo tuition
$220 p/mo for Spanish as a 2nd language

Mount View School

Pre-K - 11 / Escazú
www.mountviewcr.com
info@mountviewcr.com
Fees: Unknown

Pan American School

Pre-K - 11 / San Antonio de Belen
www.panam.ed.cr
cpcrsa@racsa.co.cr
Telephone: +506-2298-5700
Fees:
$1000 first year fee
$30 admissions exam

Pine Woods School

Pre-K - 6 / Santa Ana
No Website yet
Telephone: +506-2203-1217
Fees: unknown

Royal School

Pre-K - 11 / Escazú
www.royal.ed.cr
info@royal.ed.cr
Telephone: +506-2215-1742
Fees: Unknown

Saint Jude School

Pre-K - 6 / Santa Ana
www.stjude.ed.cr
info@stjude.ed.cr

Fees: Unknown

Saint Mary's School
Pre-K - 6 / Escazú
www.saintmary.ed.cr
info@saintmary.ed.cr
Telephone: +506-2215-2133
Fees: Unknown

Saint Paul College
Pre-K - 11 / Alajuela
www.saintpaul.ed.cr
infoesc@racsa.co.cr
Telephone: +506-2438-0824
Fees:
$375-684 tuition p/mo for 11 months

The Lincoln School
Pre-K - 11 / Heredia
www.edline.net
Telephone: +506-2247-6600
Fees:
$1,400 association fee
$600 enrollment fee
$50 matriculation
$40 misc fees
$549-910 tuition p/mo
$105-194 bus

West College Guachipelin
Pre-K - 6 / Escazú
www.westcollege.net
info@westcollege.net
Telephone: +506-2215-1384
Spanish only
Fees: Unknown

To see a listing of every school in Costa Rica go to:
www.costaricapages.com/listings/education.htm

PUBLIC SCHOOLS

Since the close of the military, Costa Rican presidents have shown their commitment towards education by funding schools and creating new programs, such as the specialized science schools .

Would I be helping or hindering my children's growth and opportunities?

Don't take my word for it. Schedule an appointment with potential colleges and employers in respectable fields. Ask them how they would respond to a potential student or employee with international experience. What I believe you will discover is that an international upbringing adds quality, diversity, and growth that no other program or school could match.

At the very least, your child will be bi-lingual (possibly tri-lingual), have successfully acclimated into another culture and way of life (huge points in both college entry and employment), and have learned life skills and experienced self-growth unmatched by a peer that remained in the United States. I would have loved it if my parents afforded had me an international upbringing.

Outside of resumés and college entry brownie points, your child will learn about nature through experiencing it with all five senses! No museum required to experience biology in Costa Rica. They will learn about world history and politics in a way that is well rounded, as opposed to a euro-centric approach. The arts are taken seriously in Costa Rica. Gone would be the days the football team acquired the monies previously allocated for the arts.

Home life could refocus around the family. The work culture is very lax, family-centric, and the cost of living low, which accumulatively could enable you to be home to play with, talk to, and shape your own children! Gone would be the days of depending on daycare or school to raise YOUR children, a dream come true for many!

Would we be able to return if we decided that it was best for the kids?

The answer to this question is very much dependent on your planning. If you are not fully committed to the idea of moving your family to Costa Rica, why not commit to a year? Save up enough emergency cash to fly everyone home and pay for at least three months of bills.

If you own your home and have gained a handsome amount of equity, you have a choice to make. You can either cash out, have your safety pile of cash, and rent in Costa Rica or you can hire a rental agency to rent your US home, and rent in Costa Rica. The risk is not equal for each option. If you choose the cash out option and Costa Rica does not work out, then you could possibly have a difficult time finding a comparable house or the same interest rate you locked into years ago.

The market, however, is unpredictable. Take the market in 2002, for example. If you had sold and moved to Costa Rica from California just before the crash, you would have likely doubled your money! Decide what is most important to you, the money upfront or the security of owning a home with potential rental income.

Work

As far as work is concerned, why not take your work with you? You would be surprised how many jobs are telecommuting friendly.[17] If your employer or your industry is not, start looking for something else that is, or start something new! CR is an excellent country to start a new

---

[17] See the Telecommuting section for more information

business in. [18]

If you packed your work and took it with you then you would not be at risk of losing your income by moving abroad or globe trotting for that matter. All the while making yourself more marketable, bi-lingual, an international specialist, or an international consultant, and so on.

Is it safe?

Safety is on every parent's mind. I don't mean to be too philosophical but what is safety? Do rules make it safe? Do low criminal statistics make it safe? Safety to me is a feeling, a vibe. I feel very safe in Costa Rica, and if I had children, I would certainly bring them here. In the United States, teen suicides, bullies, mass murders, and other evil are common occurrences.

Costa Rica has NEVER had a mass murder, a terrorist attack, or a school shooting, and suicide is nil.

Statistically, Costa Rica has higher crime in the larger cities, no surprise there. Petty theft is the most frequent crime, so if you leave valuables in your car consider it a donation.

I do not believe the statistics accurately represent the population because Ticos are not the type to report each incident.

Children are free to roam the streets playing with the neighborhood kids without fear. The culture is not fear driven here. Does that mean that bad things never happen? No, but it does mean that they don't expect it to happen. They live life more freely, what a gift that could be to your child.

---

[18] See more about starting a business in Costa Rica in the Work Hard Play Hard section

What is the cost of school?

Public schools are free and are taught in Spanish. They almost never have internationally accreditation. Private schools range from $300 per month to $1000 per month and are taught in numerous languages with varying accreditations. See the **Education** section for more.

TESTIMONIALS

A quote from a potential expat:

"When considering moving to Costa Rica, I go back and forth with the education and what my kids will do. How will they live? Half of me thinks it will absolutely be better for them in the long run to live beautifully, natural lives away from this crazy ass society. Especially in Orange County, CA. By leaving, is it taking away opportunity or is it giving them a stronger foundation? The other half of me thinks that I should stay here and move out of state someplace a little slower but in a good school district. What scares me the most is to think if we move out of California, or out of the States and walking away from our financial security, would we be able to come back if we wanted to? I hate how it all comes back to the money, but it always does."

Rona is a mother of eight and an expat living in Costa Rica for the last four years. She and her husband, Mike have traveled to Costa Rica for over ten years, often three times a year! They entered the country as expats with a fourteen year old son, Vincent. The other seven are grown up and rearing children of their own!

How did you come to the decision to leave?

Rona

After the economic crash in the States depleted much of our business, we decided there wasn't a better time to leave for Costa Rica. We had been there over 30 times, had our questions answered, and felt comfortable with the idea of living there.

It wasn't a hasty decision. We planned it out over a few years. I took Vincent to Costa Rica for two consecutive summers while Mike stayed home working to make sure he would enjoy it there. He loved it and was on board for the move.

Mike had fallen in love with the waterfalls in Costa Rica and decided to create a waterfall tour company.

Jessica

We purchased property that we had planned to use as a retirement and vacation home, but when the rentista route for immigration was set to change drastically in 2005 we decided to jump in while we still could.

What were your major concerns?

Rona

I was worried that Vinny would not be accepted and that the curriculum would not be up to par with where he was at in the US. I wanted to make sure that he could go to college wherever he wanted to.

Reality

It turns out, they used a lot of the same books as in the US and Vincent was in the right place as far as content. He did struggle at first because he didn't have the Spanish level needed to earn the grades to which he was accustom. That only lasted the first year and a half or so. He is receiving high marks now *(3 years in CR)*. He occasionally runs into trouble with specialized Spanish that he hasn't come across before. Since he is earning an A in a Spanish taught French class, I think he has come quite a ways and more importantly, he is happy!

His program currently offers the Costa Rican bachelors degree. The school is in the application process to receive their international accreditation. I don't anticipate any trouble receiving it before he graduates in four years.

Graduating from CR shouldn't weigh negatively on him because he will be bi-lingual with multicultural experiences. He does want to go to college, but is not sure if he wants to go to college in the States. I hope that he stays in CR for the first couple of years so he can be a bit more mature before he transfers to the US. I am concerned that culture shock will be much harder going back to the US than coming into CR.

Jessica

I was concerned about safety, but not because I worried about kidnapping. I was more concerned with wildlife and beach safety.

What were your considerations for schools?

Rona

I wanted him to be in class with kids from the community, not all gringos. I also wanted:
- Small class sizes
- Classes taught in both English and Spanish
- An accredited school

- School near or in Jaco where my husband works with Costa Rica Waterfall Tours.

Reality

There were not a lot of options near me, I could only interview four schools. Out of those four, I found one that I felt good about and could afford. Las Nubes is located about 400 feet away from my front door! It is accredited through CR and working towards International Accreditation. There is no religious affiliation. It costs us about $800-1000 USD at the beginning of each year for books and uniforms, then $320 per month for ten months for tuition. Ninety percent of the students are local kids and Vinny fits right in with them. The community is not exclusionary like his old school in the States. They absorbed him into the group.

One of the other schools I interviewed was Falcon. They were almost 100% gringo and all classes were taught in English with a price tag of $600 per month! Surprisingly, they are closing because of poor financial management, even with almost twice the tuition! I didn't like it there, and am very happy with the school we chose.

Vinny had problems with really cruel kids in the US, and the school systems didn't give a shit.

What extracurricular activities are there?
Rona

Our school has a soccer team, karate, and taekwondo. They also recently added a drama program.

Vinny doesn't participate in any of the school's activities. Instead, he enjoys exploring the jungle with his dad on tours, being a "mini-guide," climbing 80 foot trees *(with gear)*, solar carving, surfing, swimming, skateboarding, star-gazing with our telescope, and more recently he built a two-man sailboat from scratch!

Jessica

We homeschooled and had many activities. Each day during the kids break they got to go swimming, and sometimes we took field trips to a local waterfall.

Are you concerned about safety?
Rona

I'm not concerned about safety at all. We had visited the country with and without our children maybe 30 times before we moved here, so we knew that we were safe through experience.

Reality

I've never felt unsafe here.
Sure there is petty theft if I'm not careful, but I've never been worried about the safety of my family.

When we lived in Bejuco, I wouldn't let Vinny take the bus to school. He was only 10 years old, but it wasn't his age that concerned me, it was his level of Spanish and knowledge of the area. I was worried that he would miss his stop and not know what to do, be lost unable to communicate his needs. Now, at 14, I let him hop into taxis or ride the bus by himself. Now he has the Spanish to know how to get where he needs to go. It is not uncommon to see 5 year old children getting into taxis by themselves.

In Bejuco, I wasn't concerned at all. I let him walk to the beach by himself. But now that we live near Jaco, I won't let him because it is a tourist town. There are other factors in a tourist town. I'm more worried about the visitors and the bad apples who prey on the tourists.

We had our DSLR camera lifted from our rental car when we first arrived in Jaco. We also had a petty theft issue in a house that was unoccupied, but once it was occupied, we had no other trouble.

Jessica

Yes, but I wasn't worried about being robbed or hurt. My oldest was 9, my twins were 6, and my daughter was 4. There is four of them and only two of us. Bejuco beach is not swimmable for kids. I was worried that they would get into trouble and we would not see in time. I was also concerned about wildlife. I've had boas and tarantulas in my yard. We've had nothing but positive experiences regarding safety in CR. I have traveled all over by myself and with the kids and have never felt unsafe. But I worry every time my kids paddle out on their surf board. I worry about crocs.

Were you worried about Healthcare for your children?

Rona

No. On a view visits, my kids got bad ear infections. It was easy to be seen by a doctor. I felt they did exactly what was done in the US but there were fewer steps and less money spent. I just went to the pharmacy and the doctor there gave my kiddos the needed medicine from behind the counter. I just paid for the CHEAP medicine and was on my way. Plus, a lot of people spoke English!

Jessica

No, we weren't worried. The worst thing that our kids have gotten is swimmer's ear.

Are you less fearful in general in Costa Rica?
Rona

I'm not concerned about fear any longer. You don't hear about bad things happening here like in the US, Mexico, or Nico. Here, when something like that happens, it's all over the news, and it's a big deal because it's a rarity.

Any other advice or differences to expect in Costa Rica?
Rona

It gets dark here at 6pm, so you will need to find things for your kids to do in the dark. We bought Vinny a telescope thinking it would be a good hobby to have since there are no city lights! Also, get any books they can use for a long time because English books are hard to come by here. *The Dangerous Book for Boys* has kept him engaged and inventive for years.

Jessica

If you are moving to Costa Rica with children your number one concern should be education. After you figure out where they will go to school *then* figure out where you should live based on that. Our experience has shown that you can find a gorgeous place to live with no viable options for education.

ACCLIMATING THE CHILDREN

ADJUSTING TO THE NEW SCHOOL SCHEDULE, LANGUAGE, ACTIVITIES,
& EXPLORATION

If at all possible, plan your move so the kids have time to acclimate before school starts. Hire a private Spanish tutor for them and for you while still living in the States.

After arriving in Costa Rica sign up for intensive Spanish classes as a family for at least 2 weeks, preferably a month. You might not all be in the same class because your language levels may vary, but you will all be able to practice your Spanish with each other which will greatly assist your adjustment. If you or your spouse are struggling with the move, it will certainly reflect on your children's experience. So set yourself up for success.

ACTIVITIES

Makes sure that moving to Costa Rica is an adventure for the kids. Let them be part of the planning process. Give them assignments like, "Explore that part of the back yard and see if we can use it for something." Or if they are old enough, have them research how to compost and build a compost bin/drum/stack for you to use in a local garden. Find ways to connect their hobbies with the natural assets Costa Rica has to offer. Other activities could include:

- [ ] Creating a scavenger hunt consisting of flora and fauna, birds, and frogs known to be in the area for them to try and identify (using a wildlife guide) and take a picture. Then compare notes and see how many points they got! Reward the points with a trip to the beach or pool or waterfall!
- [ ] Bring a picnic to a nearby waterfall and enjoy the serenity.
- [ ] Go on "adventure walks" together with a wildlife guidebook, learning and identifying new plants, insects and animals each day.
- [ ] Take an "adventure night walk." Bring your headlamp and take extra care not to step on a snake. That being said, enjoy the jungle as it comes alive.
- [ ] Take Spanish lessons from the same school and have homework sessions together.
- [ ] Once a month, let a child pick somewhere new to explore within a given range. If you can afford a weekend away once a month or once every two months, this would be a great way to get to know the country.
- [ ] Google solar carving and learn a fantastic way to use the sun's energy as your paint brush by engraving the wood through burning! A much better use of the magnifying glass than killing ants! Pick up a cheap pair of welding glasses from EPA and a magnifying glass.
- [ ] Buy cheap digital cameras (possibly the disposable) and have photo contests! Winner gets to choose what's for dinner from a list of possibilities!
- [ ] Put a blanket down on the ground outside after dark and star gaze. Use an iPhone app to help you identify the constellations. You can either tell the corresponding Greek mythology stories or make up new

ones. You start the story then tag the person to your right to continue the story, and so on.

Key points to keep in mind are language acquisition, change of schedule and expectations, making new friends, and getting them connected in the community so they have a sense of purpose. For teenagers, it is of utmost importance that they make it on their own. Support any healthy hobbies or interests they express. Make sure that they have the freedom to find things that interest them.

PART V

WORK & BUSINESS

A GUIDE THROUGH THE PROCESS OF STARTING A CR OR US
BASED BUSINESSES TO BE OPERATED IN CR AND THE
CHALLENGES PRESENTED

WORK HARD PLAY HARD

**A GUIDE THROUGH THE PROCESS OF STARTING A CR OR US BASED
BUSINESSES TO BE OPERATED IN CR AND THE CHALLENGES PRESENTED**

Not Retired?

You are never too young to move to CR. It is a land for the wise, the adventurers, and the peace seekers. Herds of 20 and 30 somethings dissatisfied with the rat race have transplanted into the pura vida.

STARTUPS IN COSTA RICA

Without the hurdles of large industry that encompass entrepreneurship in the US, CR is exceedingly hospitable to small businesses.

Whether you own a business in the US, CR, or South Africa, you must satisfy a need in order to be successful.

Examine your market, (Costa Rica), and see where the gaps exist. For example, after living in Costa Rica for only months, I noticed that it was very difficult to receive online orders. I also noticed that shampoo, conditioner, and other hygiene products were far substandard than those in the States.

Each time I had a friend visiting, I sent them products I purchased off of Amazon and asked them to mule them in. This practice occurs across the expat community and is an obvious gap or need. Find a gap or need in your desired or acquired skill set and you will be on your way!

Once you decide what type of business you want to create, set out with a business and marketing plan. You will need to decide which country to register the business in, Costa Rica or your home country.

One of my businesses, EE Productions, entails filming and producing 2 minute marketing videos for adventure tours, destinations, hotels, real estate, and special events. In Costa Rica, I can stroll into a hotel or tour agency with my iPad and easily obtain an audience with the owner or manager and share what I can do for them.

In the US, it takes months of redirection, red tape, and dismissals before I may or may not successfully gain an audience with the decision maker. EE Productions is a US based business that conducts business in both the US and Costa Rica.

There is a huge market for tourism, niche group travel, retirement, medical tourism, eco-living, and self-sustaining properties just to name a few. If you were to open a hotel or tour business in Costa Rica, you would need to register it with the Costa Rican authorities.

According to the World Bank Doing Business report for 2013,[19] Costa Rica ranks 110/185 for ease of doing business. The most common complaints from expat business owners were:

---

[19] For the full report: http://www.doingbusiness.org/~/media/GIAWB/Doing%20Business/Documents/Annual-Reports/English/DB13-full-report.pdf

- Excessive bureaucracy
- Lack of infrastructure
- Inconsistent enforcement of policy
- Difficulty in receiving credit, enforcing contracts, and obtaining construction permits

On the plus side, the 2012-2013 Global Competitiveness Report places CR 57th out of 144 countries assessed.[20] Their highest scores were earned in education and innovation potential.

STEPS TO CREATING A BUSINESS IN COSTA RICA

☐ Meet with an attorney and create a Corporation, General Partnership, Limited Partnership, or Limited Liability Partnership
☐ Create a Board of Directors complete with Costa Rican Corporation minute books, or *Libros de Actas*
☐ Pay the corresponding permits (*patente or permisos*)
☐ Pay into the government tax/retirement/ health care/ workers comp program called CAJA

To form a Corporation in Costa Rica, you are required by law to have at least two individuals sign the articles of incorporation and distribute at least one share each. The law does not specify citizenship, and therefore, there is no requirement that the owners be Costa Ricans.

A three member Board of Directors is required to manage and control the affairs of the Corporation. The most commonly used roles are: President, Treasurer, and Secretary.

After you dot your i's and cross your t's, be prepared for an onsite inspection of your papers. All newly registered corporations with store front locations are visited in the first few months of operation.

---

[20]To see the full report: http://reports.weforum.org/global-competitiveness-report-2012-2013/

Oftentimes, the powers that be determine that your papers need some adjusting, and will give you instructions on what to do to correct the tremendous error.

TIP

If you plan to purchase an existing business, consider creating a new corporation. Sure, it will be more expensive than converting the shares, but since Costa Rica is not electronic, it's possible that there are open claims against the business that hasn't caught up with the Corporation yet. The papers could be clean at closing, but dirty and costly after you are responsible for footing the bill.

HIRING / FIRING TICOS

Before you decide to hire Ticos for your business, study Costa Rican labor laws carefully. They are drastically different from the laws in the US with heavy support for the worker.

For example, if your employee repeatedly no shows, sexually harasses or assaults a customer, or commits a different obvious fireable offense, you are still required to give him/her a severance package.

Pregnancy benefits are no exception. CAJA requires the employer to provide one month off prior to delivery and 3 additional months off after delivery! They receive a 100% of their wages, 50% from you and 50% from CAJA.

While lawsuits in general are much more rare here, post employment litigation is fairly common. Ticos often sue with the argument that the employer failed to comply with all labor laws and rights or did not fully pay them.

Never fire a Tico without consulting your experienced business attorney.

CAJA

http://www.ccss.sa.cr

As an employer, you are required to register your company with the Costa Rican Social Security System. You have two options: register as an individual or as an incorporated business. In order to register, you must fill out the following documents:

- ☐ The registration application form
- ☐ Copy of your ID
- ☐ Proof of address where the employees will be working (i.e. Copy of the electricity bill)
- ☐ Certificate of corporate standing *(personeria juridica)*
- ☐ Copy of the Articles of Incorporation
- ☐ Copy of the Corporate Identification document

Once you hire an employee, you are required to make certain they register with the CAJA as your employee. The reason is two fold. First, it protects your employee by providing them with medical care, disability payment, and retirement benefits. Second, you as the employer will be required to contribute 26% of their salary, (and your employee will contribute an additional 9%) to help pay for all of these benefits. CAJA to put it in US speak is social security, medicare, medical insurance, labor union, and a pension all wrapped in one nice little package of simplicity.

As mentioned above, CAJA can act similarly like a union supporting the labor force. One example is the mandated two weeks paid time off for all employees who have worked at least 50 weeks. Interestingly enough, the employee isn't allowed to choose when his vacation occurs, it's at the employer's discretion. Costa Rica also celebrates nine paid holidays and two unpaid holidays.

TICO - TIME

Plan for the fact that you will be working in Tico-time. Part of Costa Rica's draw is its slow pace and relaxed atmosphere. That fact will clearly present itself in your business experience, so plan for it.

It is all too easy to revert back to your North American workaholic business habits of stress and urgency. Don't fall back into these habits, simply plan for the tempo of the nation in your business structure. Also, plan for the low season. If your business is related to the tourism sector in any way you will experience great revenue swings month to month. Make sure you stock away a nest egg on those winning months, so you can make it through the economic droughts.

TELECOMMUTE

An increasing number of companies are seeing the win-win in telecommuting. They can lower overhead with utilities and real estate costs, and increase employee moral and productivity by allowing them to choose the environment they thrive in.

If your employer doesn't currently use telecommuters, don't worry, it doesn't mean they won't allow it. You must be savvy, and take care in how you present the offer. I recommend you read *The Work From Home Handbook* by Diana Fitzpatrick and Stephen Fishman before you pitch to your boss. The book will help polish your pitch to speak their language and address their fears or concerns before they even realize they had any.

If you don't have a job or your employer has a closed door to the option of telecommuting, then it may be time to look in another direction.

What are you experienced in? What can you bring to the table? Who would benefit from your skills? If you have worked in sales, how can you reshape yourself as an international asset.

INDEPENDENT CONSULTANT

If you have worked during your lifetime then you have experience in something. Think about what you're good at and see if you can pull together a market you can help through consultations.

There are a variety of business opportunities in Costa Rica with new business owners in every sector. These new owners need help with a variety of niches: marketing, social media, customer service practices, multi-media, international accounting, productivity, import/export, etc.

PROPERTY MANAGEMENT/ REAL ESTATE

With more and more expats looking for their retirement haven or young professionals looking for their slice of the pie, real estate has opened up dramatically in Costa Rica over the last 25 years. There was a mild cooling period just before the US recession from which CR is just starting to emerge out of. With with wealthiest and largest group of people entering their retirement years, this market is expected to boom.

The licensure does not work the same in CR as in the US. Since the CR government does not regulate this market, no licensure is required to be a real estate agent. This makes it easier to jump into the market, but beware! I strongly believe that you should perform your due diligence and research your field the same way as if you were studying for a licensure exam.   Do not expect to be signed as an exclusive buyer's or seller's agent. That's not how it typically works down here. Instead, it's a free for all. As many agents as the client desires can work on selling the same property or work with the same buyers. The only realtor that gets paid for his/her time is the one that closes the deal.

It is also strongly advised to have specialized training in Costa Rican Real Estate Law before you dub yourself an agent. In addition, every real estate transaction needs to be processed through an attorney so make sure you have an excellent bilingual lawyer to take your clients to.

Property management is also a strong market. Many Costa Ricans and expats have part time homes in CR. These homes need to be watched, maintained, and rented out to supplement income. With the humidity in Costa Rica, a house left unkept can literally rot.

TEACH ENGLISH

You can easily earn your TESOL or TEFL certificate online or in the classroom making you eligible to apply for teaching jobs around the world. Most require that you are a native English speaker, have a 120 credit hour course in either TESOL or TEFL, and some require a Bachelor's degree in any subject. In Costa Rica, most TESOL/TEFL jobs I've seen advertised are in and around the San José region.

If you are hoping to live coastal and do not see an opportunity through an agency, than you could tutor privately. It is possible to specialize in "young learner" or "business English" adding marketability and a guarantee that you teach the target audience you prefer.

I received my TESOL certificate through International TEFL and TESOL Training. I chose the 120 unit course and completed it online with my spouse. They allowed us to turn in one homework per unit since we would be completing it together. Each assignment we turned in was reviewed by our tutor, Earl. If any changes needed to be made, Earl sent it back with remarks. I have no complaints and would recommend them:

http://www.tesolcourse.com

TOURISM JOBS

Tourism is a multi-billion dollar industry. As mentioned before, the baby boomers are just beginning to enter into their retirement as the most wealthy group the world has ever seen. What do they all have in common? They all want to incorporate travel into their retirement.

Group travel has always had a healthy market and is seeing large increases in demand. What this means is that you could hop on to an established tour group as a tour director after you earn your certificate through the International Guide Academy: www.bepaidtotravel.com).

Or if you'd rather guide than direct, become a specialized guide for a niche group: LGBT, Food, Wine, Coffee, Grandparent, or Children tours to name a few. You can earn guide certification through the National Tour Association: www.ntaonline.com

If you are a more behind the scenes kind of person and have an artistic eye, you can secure work designing those flashy tourism brochures and website content.

WORK VISAS

It is no small task to secure a work visa in Costa Rica. You need to secure an employer that will sponsor and pioneer the process to demonstrate that you are filling a position that a Tico does not have the technical expertise to fill. Common work visa fields include: healthcare, IT, Biotech, and International Business.

JOBS "OFF THE BOOKS"

Under the table jobs are more often sought out by younger folks without kids. This book does not endorse working illegally, it simply acknowledges that it occurs. Under the table jobs often include: restaurant work, some bi-lingual tourism jobs (often owned by expats), flier distributer, sales, marketing, etc.

Do not expect to get paid much by working under the table. The minimum wage for legal workers in Costa Rica for an eight hour **day** is as follows:

Non-Skilled Worker: $16.39

Semi-Skilled Worker: $17.85

Skilled Worker: $18.19

Specialized Workers: $21.80

http://www.costaricalaw.com/Labor-Law/costa-rica-minimum-wage-scale-for-2013.html

VIRTUAL OFFICE 101

Telecommuting, independent contracting, creative arts, and the freedoms provided by the worldwide web, make working from any location around the world limited only by your creativity and bandwidth.[21]

In order to work from your dream location, you need to first establish the framework. This includes but is not limited to, setting up an email account, online banking, communication options, business numbers in each country code necessary, mail forwarding services, obtaining a US address, purchasing a laptop and any devices required for connection to the internet.[22]

ONLINE BANKING

Make sure that your bank allows you to bill-pay, fax wire transfer information, and charges zero or minimal currency transactions fees. At the time of writing, Charles Schwab offered a High Yield Investor Checking account with no monthly service fees or minimums, no foreign

---

[21] Internet signal strength

[22] Cable modem, wireless router, booster, or hot spot device

transaction fees, unlimited ATM fee rebates worldwide, mobile deposits from your smartphone, and FDIC insurance up to $250,000!

COMMUNICATION

Business would not exist without communication. Your business may require both local and international communication options.

Let's begin with phone communication. How is your internet connection? If it is provided through a reliable cable provider, then Skype and magicJack are excellent options for international phone communication. You simply sign up for an account, pick a number and pay one fee for a year of unlimited calling! If you maintain international clients, you can purchase a phone number with the desired country and area code for a one time annual fee.

My personal preference is Skype because of it's pleasant user interface and variety of options. I purchased a San Diego area code number for $60 USD for a year subscription. This included 3 way calling, 3 way video conferencing, and personal voicemail. As with any internet phone service, there are glitches from time to time. I've had a few instances where my voicemail did not pick up, and my client was unable to leave a message, but it is a rare occurrence.

With Skype, the customer can buy a subscription for just about any type of unlimited calling they desire: North America, Latin America, and world wide all starting at $2.99 per month!

If you have a smart phone and a local sim card installed,[23] download the Skype app. Once you are logged in and have a strong connection to the internet through either cellular or wifi, you are able to use all of your Skype features, on the go!

---

[23] See *Logistics* for more information about local sim cards

BUSINESS PHONE #S

If you plan on selling your product or service to Costa Rican residents, then you need to have a Costa Rica business number. This is more than likely going to have to be a cell phone.

In order to set up a land line, you must be a Costa Rican citizen. Some people work around by using an existing inservice landline in the office or home where they move. Instead of changing the account name, it's in the new resident simply pays the bill for said account. See *Logistics* for more on setting up your phone service.

VIRTUAL ADMIN SUPPORT

There are a variety of options available for virtual support ranging from answering services to full VAs or virtual assistants. Answering services start at just ₡80 cents a day including a friendly operator answering the phone with your company's name. Afterwards, they either forward the call or take a message and email and/or fax the message to you. ReceptionHQ has an iPhone app that allows you to change receptionist settings and diversion numbers from anywhere in the world. They offer a free 7 day trial, try them out before you leave the country and see what you think.
http://www.receptionhq.com

A virtual assistant (VA) is exactly what it sounds like, a private secretary that works from his/her home. They can answer and respond to phone calls, filter through and answer your emails and redirect only the ones that require your special attention. Common tasks they preform are: booking your travel, managing your personal and professional calendar, assisting with your social media and with blog and chat room presence.

Tim Ferriss emphasized the usefulness of VAs in his book *The 4-Hour Work Week*. One example of a VA company is EAHelp http://

www.eahelp.com. They provide an executive assistant starting with as little as 5 hours a week.

MAIL

One common problem for expats is how to handle mail. Most expats maintain a US address for credit cards, government IDs, and sometimes a business address (often a family member's address). If you have someone you trust who wants to help out, then they can receive, photograph, and email your mail to you.

If not, there are private mail services that can handle your needs. They provide two addresses, one for letters and one for packages. There is a mandatory refundable deposit and the services all deliver to your door in the San Jose area. See the individual mail carriers policies and fees for other areas. The average price is $15 USD per month which includes a few pounds worth of mail.

Keep track of your mail. You are permitted to receive $500 USD of goods every six months duty free.

A list of mail providers include:

- Aerocasillas
- Mailboxes Etc.
- JetBox
- Jetex
- Star Box
- USAMail1

ELECTRONICS

Operating from anywhere around the world requires that you are mobile, so your electronics need to reflect mobility. A laptop is much more practical than your desktop you were accustomed to if you plan to work from a variety of locations (pool, beach, time share, hotel, etc).

In Costa Rica, a cable modem is not always provided through your cable provider, so make sure you get a good one from the States. Also make sure you pick up a wifi router (if not included in your cable modem), and if you are a real techie, pick up a wifi booster. The cement walls used in home construction in CR translate to blocked wifi signal. Spend $60 USD and pick up a wifi booster (Airport Express is my favorite) and your signal will reach upstairs! Simply plug it in at the top of the stairs, and it will connect with the wifi from downstairs during configuration! 3G hot spot.

MERCHANT ACCOUNT

If you are selling goods, or hope to receive credit card payments, you will need to set up a merchant account. Paypal, Flagship ROAMpay, and Square are popular options. Read more about their features in the **Best App For Expats** section.

After the framework is created, you need to work on the environment and schedule of your desired work week. Do you have a room dedicated to work, an office or sunroom that is noise free? What do you want your work hours to be? Are you more creative and productive in the morning or late at night?

Many 8 to 5'ers are not accustomed to the variety of freedoms that working from home allows. Find out what works best for you. Experiment with your schedule until you find the best flow.

Most people feel their best when they wake up at the same time every day, shower, brush their teeth, eat breakfast, and get dressed for the day before they attempt to contribute to society. This is still true if you are working from home. Working in your PJs is possible when telecommuting but not advisable.

Do not neglect your self-care each day, and be sure to set an end time. Telecommuting does not translate into 24 hours a day working unless you let it. Just because your office is one room away or your laptop is on the night stand, does not mean you are on call.

POTENTIAL BUSINESSES MARKETS IN COSTA RICA

- Import / Export business
- Beauty shop with US quality products
- Destination Wedding Planner
- Expat mail / courier service

TAXES, CORPS, & BANKING

TRICKS FOR CURRENCY CONVERSION, INSIGHTS ON TAXES AND REPORTING, & AN INTRODUCTION TO COSTA RICAN BANKING

"PAYING THE MAN"

The Costa Rican government takes getting paid seriously. Make certain you are on time filing your corporate tax returns no later than December 15th with your fiscal year running from October 1st - September 30th. Tax rates vary from 10-30 percent of your net profits. There are a variety of different types of taxes. Take for example how tough they are on cars without up-to-date Marchamo *(tax)*: they pull you over and impound the car! In the US, you would get a ticket and sent on your way.

CORPORATION TAX

On April 1st, 2012 CR decided to celebrate April Fool's day by passing a new annual taxation on all corporate entities registered in CR. The tax was created to support the required administrative jobs in order to maintain the records of an ever increasing list of corporations. Since corporations are created for operations such as buying a recreation vehicle or house, this tax should bring in a fat check and deter some people from creating unneeded corporations. The amount of the tax is 180,330 Colones ($358 USD) for active corporations and 90,175 Colones ($179 USD) for inactive corporations.

The government determined this rate by taking the base salary of a government employee and charging the active corporation half and the inactive corporation a quarter of their salary. The tax is due on January 1st of every year.

If you sell goods and services deemed anything other than "basic necessities," you must charge a 13% sales tax *(impuesto de ventas)*. Furthermore, if those goods are imported tack on applicable tariffs.[24] To figure out what your tariffs and import/export taxes will be visit http://www.dutycalculator.com. Which is why Tide laundry detergent is $20 for a tiny bottle!

This is another area to have a well informed attorney/ CPA. Most business owners have two or three lawyers in varying specialties. Taxes can get complicated and may become even more complicated soon.

INTERNATIONAL TAX

There are a variety of proposals being thrown around to create an international tax or tax on a company/ individual's worldwide income. The provocation for change is international multi-million dollar companies including Google, Starbucks, and rich individuals, who have given up their US citizenship just before receiving a large sum of money from an investment or inheritance while utilizing international shields to dodge paying taxes.

---

[24] The amount of the tariff is based on the International Convention on the Harmonized Commodity Description and Coding System, or Partida Arancelaria, as it is called locally. See http://www.wcoomd.org for more information.

The United States and other developed countries have realized that without the taxation of theses mega offshore companies and rich individuals, they are loosing billions of dollars in taxes.

From May to June of 2013, the US saw more people emigrate than any other full year in the history of the United States, over 1,000 people. This shift is believed to be due to a 2010 law entitled the Foreign Account Tax Compliance Act (FATCA)[25] which is scheduled to be implemented by 2014. The FATCA will make it 'legal' for the US to bully financial institutions around the world into providing account numbers of clients who hold US citizenship. This information is then sent to the good old IRS. It doesn't stop there! The US will be able to direct your foreign bank to withhold and remit taxes from any income deposited by the client! Since you are already paying taxes on income earned in Costa Rica, this would be double taxation, hence many people are deciding to renounce their citizenship.

As of this writing, there are no taxes on worldwide income. By definition, an international tax would create double taxation. If the US is successful in creating it, they can add double taxation to Washington D.C.'s taxation without representation faux pa. Keep your eye on this issue if you own an international business or have assets in a foreign bank.

FREE ZONE

Free Trade Zone Law

This benefit will be reshaped in 2015. At the current moment, your company may be eligible to receive 100% exemptions on: import duties, raw materials, export taxes, and income taxes! The CR Free Zone is designed to bring in more foreign development businesses in the

---

[25]FATCA info: http://www.irs.gov/Businesses/Corporations/
ForeignAccountTaxComplianceAct_LegalDocumentsandNoticeInformation

tourism and reforestation sectors. However, if the pending controversial US tax law is passed, then a 15% tax will be assessed on all revenue generated from companies working under the Free Trade Zone Law. Sounds like it would defeat the purpose and could potentially send businesses packing up shop to reopen in neighboring Panama where benefits are ample.[26]

BUSINESS BANKING

As a business owner, you will be required to open a Costa Rican bank account to pay taxes and manage your books. Keep the following paperwork handy:

- Copies of your passport
- Your Corporate paperwork
- Article of powers
- Permits, *permisos*
- Copy of your lease (storefront)

Better yet, take your incorporation attorney and have him/her assist you in opening the account. Costa Rican attorneys are usually very happy to lend a hand since they know the process and exactly what the bank needs. The help with Spanish is also a great asset. More than likely, the bank will be a short stroll away!

Online banking is available and widely used. If you wish to make transfers, you'll need to pick up an OTT device which is a random number generator that provides security while accessing and moving your funds.

---

[26] From 2003-2010 Costa Rica enticed 30% more businesses investors than their neighbors, Panama did. In 2011 Panama leveled the playing field.

EXPERIENCE

Mike Marino, of www.CostaRicaWaterfallTours.com shares his story becoming an *Banco Nacional* client.

"It was a fairly straightforward process. My account was set up in one day. I brought a Tico friend who acted as an interpreter *(Banking Spanish is a lot different from conversational Spanish)*, my Corporation paperwork, my permisos *(permits)*, and a copy of my lease. I didn't realize that I needed a copy of my passport, so I told the clerk I would go get the copy and be back. When I re-entered the bank 30 minutes later, the clerk was waiting for me my documents still spread across his desk. He hadn't taken anyone from the line for 30 minutes, instead he sat happily waiting for my return! I sat down passport copy in hand and we finished our business. Worked out great for me, but if I were one of the people waiting in line I would have lost it!"

WHICH BANK IS BEST?

The best bank depends on what you value most: quality customer service, short lines, bilingual staff, government backed insurance, or ease of use. The first two banks mentioned are government owned/run. That fact hits you in the face when you walk through the doors. Take a ticket and have a seat... The plus side is they are government insured and since they have the same boss, so to speak, if you bank with one you can access your account from the other. It's like two adjacent bicycle spokes leading to the same center. The private banks do a better job with customer service, have a better chance of employing a bi-lingual banker, and have speedy service. The downside is they are not government insured, and their system is not foreigner friendly.

Banco Nacional
- ☑ Most popular bank with Ticos
- ☑ Government backed/ run
- ☑ Government insured online transaction post faster than the other guys
- ☑ Long lines
- ☑ Sometimes apathetic customer service, it's like going to the DMV
- ☑ Free Transfers

Bank of Costa Rica
- ☑ Government backed/ run
- ☑ Government Insured Sometimes apathetic customer service, it's like going to the DMV
- ☑ Free Transfers

Bank of San José
- ☑ Privately run
- ☑ No insurance
- ☑ Good customer service
- ☑ Attentive to lines, do their best to minimize wait times
- ☑ Can take up to 3-4 hours to certify funds for a transfer
- ☑ Transfer fee

Banco Popular
- ☑ Privately run
- ☑ No insurance
- ☑ Good customer service

☑ Attentive to lines, do their best to minimize wait times
☑ Transfer fee

ACCEPTING CREDIT CARDS

There is no doubt that Costa Rican merchant accounts kick you in the gut with fees that hover in the 7-8% range! In the US, merchant fees range from 0.5%-2.75%. This is the reason businesses often charge $5+ to accept credit card payments, or offer a cash discount. If your company is US based, you can use a US merchant. To see the best rated merchants view the **Best Apps for the Expat** Section.

US TAXES

It doesn't take a tax profession to recognize that the US wants their cut of the pie. Even though you have left the States, they will still tax you. Some expats have given up their citizenship in an effort to avoid paying taxes to a country they do not live in. If your worth is greater than $622,000 and you gave up your citizenship, you may be pursued by the IRS for tax evasion. The US has even gone so far as to create an Expatriation Tax which requires the expat who has renounced their citizenship to pay taxes for 10 years after they are no longer a US citizen! In the last quarter, over 1600 people emigrated from the US the highest record in the history of the US, as mentioned above in the **International Tax** section. Since the US is losing people from the highest tax brackets to other countries, they have created a new law to deter others from emigrating. It would not allow the expat to reacquire their citizenship should they experience a change of heart! Seems like the government holds a grudge!

You can file your US tax return through the U.S. Embassy in San José or mail it.[27]

---

[27] Go to the IRS website, U.S. Citizens and Resident Aliens Abroad section for more information.

FOREIGN EARNED INCOME EXCLUSION
for US citizens

A potential break in the aggressive US tax requirements is the Foreign Earned Income Exclusion. In order to qualify, you must be a US citizen, your tax country must be outside of the US, be a "bona fide resident" of Costa Rica *(or other non-US country)*, and have spent ≥330 full days there during a period of 12 consecutive months. The days are in total, they do not have to be consecutive, and are not reset on January 1st. In any 12 month span, you cannot have spent more than 34 days outside of CR to qualify.

If you qualify, you won't have to pay any taxes on income up to $97,600. You may also qualify to deduct foreign housing costs.[28] The annual cap for the housing exclusion is $29,280 or 30% of the maximum Foreign Earned Income Exclusion. Remodeling, decorating, and furnishing is not included.

If you qualify for the exclusion, it doesn't mean you don't have to file taxes. You are required to file if you made more than $9,750 in world-wide income. You may not pay a dime, but Uncle Sam wants to keep an eye on you.

The most popular tax forms for the expat are the standard 1040, Form 2555-Foreign Earned Income Exclusion, and the From 1116-Foreign Tax Credit.

The rules for this exclusion are not simplistic. I would recommend using a CPA or other tax professional who specializes in expatriate taxes.[29] This section is in no way to be used as the sole reference for tax guidance. It's simply a gringo's take on expat taxes as best as I can

---

[28]For more on foreign earned income exclusion: http://www.irs.gov/Individuals/International-Taxpayers/Foreign-Earned-Income-Exclusion

[29] Publication 54, Tax Guide for U.S. Citizens and Resident Aliens Abroad.

understand. *See the resource directory for CPAs and attorneys vouched for by expats.*

TIP

"A word of advise regarding lawyers. Don't do business with an attorney that has a fancy office and high profile clients. He will suck you dry and do nothing for you. Find a simple lawyer who speaks English and ask lots of questions BEFORE buying anything. After speaking with the lawyer, pay their fee, thank them. Then find two more attorneys and ask the same questions. If you get a consensus of two out of three then you will have a basis to make a decision. No matter how smart you are in the States, the legal codes are completely different in CR. A couple of hundred dollars is well worth the saved aggravation."

~ Sandra Brooks, Expat Consultant
smbapr@yahoo.com

HOW TO LIVE FOR FREE

TEACHING YOU TRICKS AND THE INNER WORKINGS OF THE SYMBIOTIC RELATIONSHIP THAT
EXISTS IN OVERSEAS LIVING AND THE BARTERING SYSTEM

Living for free is not a myth or a gimmick. People are living rent free and sometimes room and board free across the globe. This lifestyle can be temporary for those who are investigating areas to buy a home, all the while saving some serious coin! It can also serve those who are in a financial riff, or it can open up an entire new concept of life for folks who aren't attached to things or a location: true nomads. Living rent free can also serve those who are passing through on their journey. Whatever the reason, whatever your situation, it is possible so unless you are attached to your things, it's crazy not to consider!

HOUSE/HOTEL/PET SITTING

Exactly as it sounds. If you are a house, hotel, or pet sitter, you would watch and maintain the property and animals exactly as the owner specifies. If you do your homework right, this type of arrangement is a win win and can be an excellent way to save money while experiencing life in a new area!

There is a huge range of responsibilities from one job to another. Which is why it is extremely important to ask all of the right questions to get all of the information, rules, and expectations out in the open before you commit to any job. Your tasks could range from watching a house and watering plants, to a rigorous pet activity and care program that requires something of you every couple of hours. Below are some examples of websites that advertise care-taking jobs. While options in CR exists, none of the sites exist solely for Costa Rica, and their inventory constantly turns over.

Professional Association of Innkeepers International
Range from $89-$1299 p/year depending on membership selection
www.innkeeping.org

Caretakers Gazette
$30 p/year www.caretaker.org

Trusted House Sitters
$49 for three months
$64.00 for 6 months
$79.00 12 months
www.trustedhousesitters.com

Word of Mouth & Part-Time Expat
Keep your eyes and ears open for opportunities to help other expats keep their home safe while you can score a rent-free situation!

Like anything worth achieving, you will have to put in effort to reach your goal. After all, living for free is a pretty epic goal. There will be others competing with you. The first job is often the hardest to land because you lack experience and pertinent references. The key to success is to look each sitting opportunity as a job interview, only the interviewer is asked as many questions as the interviewee (you).

Your profile on the service you choose is the equivalent to your resume. If you don't put in effort here don't bother subscribing. Remember, these home and pet owners are looking for a stranger to welcome into their home when they aren't going to be there! Don't sound like a robot, be yourself in a respectable way and show passion. Let them get to know you through your profile.

Include examples that display how responsible you are, your hobbies, your cleanliness, pet enthusiasm, experience, and what you can do for them. Don't just say you like dogs, make sure and use examples demonstrating how much you care for animals. If you have horse, gardening, or farming experience, say so. If you haven't worked as a house/ pet sitter abroad, but have done so for family and friends, include that experience with your loved ones as your references. If you have experience with www.couchsurfing.org, make sure to include that along with your user name, then the homeowners can read your reviews on each site. When in doubt, ask for previous bosses, landlords, and even teacher to vouch for your trustworthiness and reliability.

Everyone has a special set of skills, if yours happens to be handy work, then mention it. Homeowners will feel better knowing their home will be cared for if something breaks while they are away. If you have gardening skills, marketing skills, computer skills, alternative energy skills, list them. You never know how your skills could benefit the homeowner. After all, the goal here is a mutually beneficial relationship!

Once you find a job you want to apply for, you have a chance to send a brief message along with your profile for their review. Treat this message like a cover letter. A brief introduction to what you can do for them, why their house is the job you want, and why they should hire you over other prospective sitters. Make sure to be passionate and real. Show your personality in a professional way.

Speaking of professionalism, makes sure to respond quickly and professionally to each email correspondence. Write their name at the top, use full sentences, and always end your message with something to the effect of, "I appreciate your time and consideration."

Hesitation may cost you excellent housesitting opportunities. If the house is in a desirable location, it will often get filled the same day it posts. Setting up alerts for your desired location could be the most important thing you do with your service.

Once you have captured a homeowners interest and have answered their questions or concerns, don't neglect your own. You need to ask the right questions to insure the position is a good fit for you. Ask the owner:

- Is it ok to have guests?
- How long can the pet/house can be left alone? (You may wish to explore to a nearby town for the weekend)
- Is there a vehicle you can use?
- What is public transit like near them?
- How far away is the nearest grocery store?
- Will you have access to the internet?
- Is there warm water?
- Are there any rules you need to abide by?

MASTERING HOUSE / PET SITTING

In order to be an excellent house/ pet sitter, all that's required is to use common sense and follow the owner's requests. Remember you are a guest, so make sure you return the home in *better* condition than when you left it. Wash the linens you used, make sure the house is tidy, and if you want brownie points, leave something homemade in the fridge for their arrival home with a note so they know you made it especially for them.

Pay attention to the owner's requests. If the owner said to leave the mail in a certain area, make sure and neatly place the mail in the designated area. If they want you to check in via email every so often, make sure and set an alarm in your calendar to do so. If you respect their wishes and do more than the minimum required, then you will have an unending list of positive references and this rent-free lifestyle will open up for you.

WORK EXCHANGE

One method to try an area in Costa Rica as a potential home is through a work exchange. www.Helpx.net is a website where you can search for places to work in exchange for free room and board. (On the flip side of that once you do own a home, you can host workers through the site to help you remodel, or advertise a new business in exchange for room and board).

Take time to build a good profile advertising what skills you have to share. Next, search the country where you desire to work, and the type of work that you want to do.

For example, I searched Costa Rica and organic farm stay. This resulted in a list of organic farm owners who were looking for some extra help in exchange for room and board.

The range of work possibilities is extensive. Examples of work projects include: help with new construction, marketing, refurbishing a boat, gardening, cooking, teaching English, farming, housekeeping, concierge, working with horses, etc.

The most common arrangement I noted was 20 hours of work in exchange for free room and board. You must clarify your specific deal with the owner because every situation is unique. Some work exchanges are full-time in exchange for free room and board and an additional stipend.

The above mentioned Caretakers Gazette also offers work exchanges for a small stipend and free room and board. Most frequently, I have observed work as caregivers, handy-person work, and live-in hotel managers.

COUCH SURFING

Couch surfing is not just a way to describe sleeping on your cousin's couch any longer. Now, it is an entire genre of travel. People of all ages travel around the world meeting Couch Surfers from each of the countries they've traveled.

www.CouchSurfing.org is a site whose slogan is, "Changing the world one couch at a time." To experience this new way of travel, all you need to do is sign up to create a profile. There you can decide whether you would like to potentially host travelers, show them around, or meet them for coffee and exchange stories. You are never required to host people even if your profile says that you can. You can search for potential hosts or for those looking for a place to stay in your area. If you find a "couch" you would like to surf, you simply write to them. Tell them why you would like to stay, showing that you read their profile, and ask if there is anyway you could crash there during the time that you will be in the area. Even though it's called "couch" surfing, oftentimes your host has a spare bedroom you can have all to yourself! The sleeping situation is listed in the profile of the potential host. I have couch surfed in Canada, St. Lucia, and the United States. I have hosted surfers many times in Costa Rica and had great experiences! I now have places around the world to stay!

Couch surfing is not a long term solution as the average stay is 2 nights. It is a great way to travel around CR looking for the region that best suits you, and gathering information and advice from locals and expats who have already made the move. My profile is shown as an example *on the next page.*

BOOK TO READ

- *Working Abroad* by Johnathan Reuvid
- *The Work From Home Handbook* by Diana Fitzpatrick and Stephen Fishman

PART VI

HEALTHCARE & GOLDEN YEARS

AN INTRODUCTION TO SOCIALIZED MEDICINE, SUPPLEMENTAL
INSURANCE, RETIREMENT IN COSTA RICA, & THE PART-TIME EXPAT

HEALTHCARE

AN INTRODUCTION TO SOCIALIZED MEDICINE, LESS RED TAPE,
EXCELLENT ACCESS TO CARE, AND SUPPLEMENTAL PRIVATE
INSURANCE OPTIONS

Health, according to Merriam-Webster, is *"the condition of being sound in mind, body, or spirit."* Making the move to the first ranked happiest place on earth two years running may be the best thing you can do for your health and longevity![30]

Healthcare is quirky and each individual will carry a unique comfort level to acquire peace of mind. You will read that managing your healthcare can range from no insurance *(pay the cheap out of pocket rates as illness occurs)* to a combination of public, private, and international healthcare insurances. Each plan carries a corresponding price tag and peace of mind.

---

[30] Happy Planet Index

PREVENTION

A few Tico friendly, health-seeking, illness prevention techniques include:

◉Eat like the locals and your weight and cholesterol should see a natural drop. *(i.e. casados, pinto gallo)*
◉Take daily walks through your new natural oasis and see your mood, energy level, bone density, Vitamin D levels, and health improve.
◉Replace sugar drinks and beer with fresh coconut water (agua de pipa) and smoothies made from the ridiculously delicious produce.

CARE

After talking to numerous on the fence expats-to-be, one of the major concerns was healthcare. For those entering their 50s, 60s, and 70s, they have seen the changes in US healthcare over the last 20 years. Mass media proclaims that government controlled healthcare is detrimental to your health. Stating that you will wait in long lines with no availability for needed surgeries for months. As with many things we hear on the news, this just isn't true. It's another scare tactic employed by the media.

With the United States healthcare in complete flux and Medicare slated to run out of funding, I wonder whether or not the potential expat should be more concerned over healthcare in the US versus healthcare in Costa Rica. As of 2010, 49.9 million Americans were uninsured! That's 16.3% of the total population!

Sometimes it just comes down to comfort level. If you've had the same cardiologist or family practitioner for years, you have a history and a trust that has been courted. Costa Rica will bring you back to the drawing board. Which is why I highly recommend you interview doctors during your "try before you pry" time. Make an appointment and interview specialists that are applicable to your needs.

INTERVIEW YOUR DOCTOR:

☐ Where did they completed schooling?

☐ Are they board certified? *(All physicians are licensed but not all are board certified)* If so, in what specialty?

☐ How do they complete their continuing education and stay current with medicine?

☐ How many patients have they had with my particular ailment/ condition?

☐ How can you reach them outside of office hours? Cell phone number?

☐ Do they respond to calls during office hours?

☐ If they are out of town, who fills in for them?

☐ What is their philosophy of healthcare?

☐ Is the location where we are meeting their only location or are there others?

☐ How do they handle billing?

After you have collected all of your information with at least three physicians (preferably those you have been referred to), decide what questions and answers hold the most stout with you and score them accordingly. Don't forget to weigh in heavily with your comfort level and rapport with your future physician.

QUALITY

The Costa Rica health care system is actually ranked HIGHER than the US healthcare system by the World Health Organization (WHO), even though it's budget is a fraction of that of the United States. It is ranked #1 in Latin America! Both WHO and the United Nations Development Program (UNDP) have placed Costa Rica in the top ranking for long life expectancy, higher than the United States. In fact, the Nicoya Peninsula is considered one of the "Blue Zones" of the world.

A blue zone is a term used by Dan Buettner in his book *The Blue Zones: Lessons for living longer from people who lived the longest* to identify a geographic area where people are living measurably longer lives. He attributes the increased health to overlapping traits he found in each of the blue zones: family-centricity, fewer smokers, predominantly plant-based diet, moderate physical activity, social engagement, and legumes.

Many hospital facilities in Costa Rica are internationally accredited by the Joint Commission International (JCI). The most well known hospital boasting superior care is CIMA, a private hospital located in Escazú. Just behind CIMA in popularity is Clinica Biblica and Hospital La Catolica. There are numerous bi-lingual doctors available, many of who are US board certified and received their training in the US.

CAJA

The Caja Costarricense de Seguro (Social Security Administration) has provided healthcare to residents while sharpening and improving it's services for over 70 years. Initially, the program was geared only towards wage-earning residents, but over time, dependents were added and the CCSS absorbed responsibility for all 29 pubic hospitals and healthcare in it's entirety.

They included the indigenous and mountaineers by launching the Programa de Salud Rural (Rural Health Program) so that primary care could extend out to those off the grid.

In 1993, laws were passed to assure that the CCSS would keep the people's needs at the forefront. The laws created health-boards with individuals elected to represent: consumers, social security, employers, and social organizations.

Residents are required to purchase a plan through CAJA. The rate is based on your age and seems to range from $50-70 p/month.

CAJA FROM THE STREETS *information provided by Sandra Brooks, an expat for over 9 years and insurance representative*

Once you have a CAJA plan, you are assigned a district. If you need to schedule an appointment or be seen by a doctor, you must start at your EBAIS *(a neighborhood clinic)*. They do not make appointments, it's on a first come first, serve basis. In busy towns, you must go to the clinic early and stand in line to get a space in the appointments for the day. Because of this, many people opt to see private physicians *(who are also CAJA doctors)* by appointment then the doctor writes the prescription on a CAJA order allowing the patient to fill their prescriptions by using their CAJA. They also reserve CAJA for major illness or emergencies.

Most people who need to be seen the same day, go to the hospital. I had to go to the hospital after getting stung by a devious scorpion that was hiding in my kitchen cabinet on Christmas Day. I was seen within the hour. The hospital staff called groups of 6 back to be seen by the doctor. After the physician prescribed a bunch of pills and three injections, I waited in the pharmacy for my shots and pills to be filled. The rooms were not clean in my local hospital and the conditions were cramped.

If you need to be admitted to the hospital while using your CAJA, you must go to your assigned county hospital *(similar to the rules in the USAs HMO plans)*. If your regional hospital cannot treat your illness or a specialty treatment is required, then you are assigned a providence hospital.

Public hospitals have 6 beds to a room without curtains to provide privacy. Only one visitor at a time is allowed in the room during visiting hours.

In order to keep my sanity and not appear as an arrogant American, I have found a way to join the middle class Costa Ricans who pay out of pocket and forgo the system they too are paying for through their salaries.

One major difference with hospitals in Costa Rica is they are not obligated to treat you. You must have a minimum deposit to get in and are required to pay the bill in full upon check out.

If you are considering making CAJA your primary insurance, tour the facilities in each region where you may be assigned before choosing a permanent place to live.

~ *Sandra Brooks, Expat Consultant*
smbapr@yahoo.com

OPT OUT

Healthcare is cheap, just pay out of pocket! This is the most common path for perpetual tourists. They can't pay into the CAJA without a Cedula card, so their options are restricted to opting out and pay out of pocket as needed, or to purchase a private or international plan.

Interestingly enough, I have found that most people with pensions and thereby a pensianado resident are purchasing supplemental insurance on top of their CAJA, and those people without pensions, (perpetual tourists), are opting to pay as they go since there isn't a lot of extra cash flow.

If you are concerned about cost, you are free to call the hospital where you would go, and ask them the costs for a variety of procedures.

They have a fee schedule and will tell you the cost and the minimum you need to bring to get through the doors.

PRIVATE INSURANCE

If you are wary to rely on the Costa Rican healthcare system (even though they're ranked higher than the US), are a part time expat, or just wish to have supplemental insurance to guarantee fast care, then you should look into supplemental private health insurance.

There are a variety of options ranging from Cigna to Costa Rican INS.

INS

Don't qualify for CAJA and don't want to spend an arm and a leg on international insurance? INS is the private sector counterpart of the CAJA. The benefits of membership are plainly seen with higher efficiency and speedy access to procedures and specialists. If you are a member of the Association of Residents of Costa Rica (ARCR) you can save 10% on your rate! The ceiling of this plan is fairly low at $17,500 per year of paid expenses. However, take into consideration the low cost of care, plus you can choose any doctor that you want! The plan does not cover pre-existing conditions. INS will pay for 80% of your prescription medicine, exams, hospitalization, and treatment. Most importantly it pays 100% of surgeon and anesthetist fees. Premiums vary greatly due to age and sex: $250 - $1,400 per year. *Sandra Brooks* had INS for a year but cancelled after finding a private insurance that would cover them in both the US and in Costa Rica with a $1 million a year coverage.

INS offers both regional and global insurance plans. They also offer home and auto insurance.

Charlene and Diego, expats that live on the Central Pacific Coast, say they are very happy with INS. They recently used it for an outpatient procedure preformed at CIMA and had nothing but good things to say for the care and facilities. They also compared the INS rate to other private insurances like Cigna, stating INS was the way to go.

INTERNATIONAL HEALTHCARE
Cigna

Since age is important, do not lag on this decision. Once you decide what plan is best for you, start the application. You will pay less premiums and lock in at a better rate. If you wait until your move, you may have more difficulty especially if you are 64+ years of age.

Above, and on the next page, is a quote from Cigna for a 54 year old woman with a $1,500 deductible. The following page provides a partial breakdown on what her money buys.

EXPAT EXPERIENCE

Sandra Brooks is an expat who has lived in CR for over 9 years. She has worked with a variety of insurances and when she settled on the best plan, she referred so many people the insurance company has designated her as a representative. I asked Sandra to give me two quotes for insurances that are commonly used in CR.

~ Sandra Brooks, Expat Consultant
smbapr@yahoo.com

Morgan White Administrators International

Is recommended for healthy families who want great care while minimizing cost. With this plan, you will still be covered if you return to the US.

New World Plan

A moderately priced plan that does not require underwriting. If you have a pre-existing condition, you can still purchase the policy. That particular condition will be excluded from coverage but if your concern is accidents and infectious diseases, you will be covered!

- A $2,000 deductible will cost a retired couple of 65 & 58 $491 per month in total. A family of four ages: 33, 30, 5, and 2 would cost $222 per month.
- Plus *New World* has a special arrangement with Clinica Biblica in San José and Liberia for patients to receive $1,000 off of the deductible.

Sandra has personal experience using the insurance:

"My husband became ill just after switching to New World Insurance. He was in and out of the hospital. We paid our deductible once and that was it. In one month, New World paid out over $20,000 in medical expenses. When Richard passed, the company paid for my travel expenses for repatriation of remains even though I had him cremated."

Other International Insurance providers include:

Bupa: www.bupa.com

HTH Worldwide: www.hthworldwide.com Prices range from $62 p/mo - $3,479!

BROKERFISH

www.brokerfish.com

This is a search option that you can use just like searching for car insurance. You enter in the ages of your family members and your desired international coverage. The most expensive factors seem to be whether or not you wish to have coverage in the US and whether or not you want to include emergency evacuation.

TRAVEL INSURANCE

If you do not stay put for longer than 6 months at a time then travel insurance may be your best option. It also might be the ideal choice for the part-time expat, see more in the **Part Time Expat** section.

MEDEX

www.medexassist.com

I asked for a quote for two US citizen travelers ages 63 and 48 set to travel to Costa Rica for exactly 5 months. The cost for the 63 year old was $710.62 for their *Choice Plan*, and $517 for their *Global Plan.* The 48 year old could expect to pay $382.91 for *Choice* and $517 for *Global*. For 5 months coverage the two would pay a combined $1,093.53-$1,034 *($218.71-$206.80 per month)*.

This quote was conducted for both the medical evacuation and medical insurance coverages.

An added bonus going this direction for medical insurance is you also gain coverage for personal belongings, luggage, trip cancellation, and sometimes theft. Make sure the coverage that you choose has coverage inside of the US if you think you may need to return within the given time period. Many insurances omit the US due to the inflated healthcare expenses.

PHARMACIES

Personally speaking, I've had a handful of ear infections and other minor ailments. With farmacías at every major corner, I never had to seek out a physician. I simply walked in and explained my symptoms, in Spanish. The pharmacist asked a few follow up questions and sometimes looked into my ears or felt my glands. Then he/she sold me a handful of pills with directions. I happily paid the small fee for the medicine and was grateful to save time from a doctors appointment and waste a copay. I usually left the farmacía with a $10-20 USD hole in my wallet. Not bad.

I also decided to have my blood work done. For a basic panel, I paid $40 USD without using insurance or CAJA. If I wanted to screen for ovarian cancer, rheumatoid factor, kidney function, spleen, liver, and a slew of other tests, I could pay approximately $230 USD for an all inclusive under the hood panel.

Neighbors of mine made the journey to the hospital in Quepos for a painful urinary tract infection that wouldn't resolve. They were well taken care of and it didn't cost them more than $50 USD to see an ER physician, have blood work, and a sonogram performed. To top it off, their wait time did not exceed 15 minutes!

MALPRACTICE

Some potential expats are nervous about medicine that doesn't have the backing of a billion dollar medical malpractice insurance industry. After all, there is always risk involved with medical care, and if human error was made then it would be nice if your loved ones were covered. Let me explain the differences between the malpractice industry in the US and Costa Rica.

UNITED STATES

In the United States, medical malpractice is an industry in itself. There are tort lawyers clawing at pharmaceuticals, insurance companies for health care professionals, and litigators that make sure the providers are insured. The most expensive cost a US based physician has is medical malpractice insurance. That cost exceeds rent in most cases.

In the US, malpractice is pursued in civil courts with four main ingredients to prove fruitful:

1. A duty was owed- a healthcare provider or hospital has a legal duty when they undertake the treatment of a patient.
2. A duty was breached- the medical provider did not perform to the standard of care.
3. The breach caused an injury.
4. Damage occurred.

COSTA RICA

Medical malpractice claims are processed differently from the very beginning. For example, malpractice claims run through a mixture of civil and criminal law with criminal proceedings as the usual outcome!

Criminal codes: Homicidio Culposo (art. 117) and Lesiones Culposas (art. 128) represent when an act results in the patients death and when the act results in an injury.

In order to prove medical malpractice, three elements must be present:

1. "The fault or omission (voluntary or involuntary) which produced the death or injury and which was foreseeable and avoidable in the standard duty of care in the medical profession.
2. The act resulted in damage to the patient.
3. The proximate cause is a direct consequence of the fault or omission committed by the healthcare provider." [31]

As with all bureaucratic proceedings, the going is slow. Medical malpractice lawsuits are not common and can take an eternity to wind through the judicial system. The pot of gold on the other side is also significantly smaller than comparable US damages.

---

[31] As cited from www.CostaRicaLaw.com

AVAILABILITY

I cannot make an all inclusive statement regarding wait times. Each region, each facility, is different. Each day a facility could have drastically different wait times from the next. Instead, I share with you experiences from expat friends of mine.

Paul, a cedula carrying resident of the Central Pacific Coast has used his CAJA for his step daughter. He went to his local doctor's office and reports that he had very little wait time, was satisfied with the doctor and care performed and had no copay! He was also given the medicine that was prescribed right there in the office with no additional fee!

When Paul moved to Costa Rica he was a single man who obtained his cedula through pensianado. Now happily living with a new partner and her child, he was able to add both of them to his pensianado and his medical insurance, or CAJA. How much extra did it cost to add two dependents? Zero! He pays $59 USD a month through the Association for Costa Rica Residents right from his CR bank account quarterly. Paul has no taxes in Costa Rica and enjoys the new life he chose for himself in the pura vida.

MEDICAL TOURISM

Three per cent of the *world*'s population travels internationally for medical treatment![32] That's roughly 211,710,000 people! Patients Beyond Borders, an organization that publishes international medical travel guidebooks, reported that the medical tourism industry produces $40 billion a year in business.

Patients requiring elective, non-elective, and dental procedures are heading to Costa Rica. Procedures are often less than half the cost in the United States.

---

[32] IPK International Survey

The medical tourism industry capitalizes where the US lacks. Companies like Healthcare Beyond Boundaries www.healthbase.com commonly offer all inclusive packages with post-op R&R stays at luxurious guest houses overlooking exotic water or jungle to assist and encourage their rapid recuperation. All of this for a fraction of the cost of the corresponding US surgery where the patient gets a script for Percocet and a kick in the rump on the way out the door.

On the flip side, Costa Rica has also become well known for organ transplants. A little too well known. Costa Rica is now on the radar as a premiere organ trafficking location. If you google organ transplant in Costa Rica, you are sure to run into an ugly problem here in paradise.

Costa Rican officials are well aware of the problem and have received a generous load of bad media after the arrest of Dr. Francisco José Mora for allegedly heading up an organ trafficking market in San José.

There is a bill in the works to outlaw organ donation by non-relatives unless they are found to be genuinely motivated. It is already illegal to take money or advertise for donors. So, I'm not sure how this new law could be enforced nor how intent could be deciphered, but watch for this new theoretical bill in the next year.

BOOKS

Patients Without Borders: Everybody's Guide to Affordable, World-Class Healthcare

RETIRED LIFE

REINVENTING YOU, GETTING CONNECTED, FALLING BACK IN LOVE
WITH LIFE

Live in a place where as your age increases so does your level of respect from the community

One size does not fit all, nor does one way of retiring fit every retired individual. This transition is not to be taken lightly. Just as your transition into adolescence, adulthood, and possibly parenthood were taken seriously so to should your transition into your wisest stage.

Greenwich Study
Happy Retirees:
Were Intellectually stimulated
Were Not addicted to TV
Were socially active (more important than having kids)
Were healthy
Had a significant other
Had enough money

Considering a move to another country is an excellent time to sit and reevaluate the person that you are today. Your life experiences have shaped you and groomed you to be who you are, don't base your decisions on the person you were in the 60s, 70s, or 80s. Instead, decide what is important to you now? Reshape your life based on your new priorities.

PRIORITIES

I'm giving you homework! Create a priority chart, listing no fewer than 15 priorities. Next to each priority, rate it's importance by writing a number 1 - 10, 1 being the most important, 10 being the least.

It is very possible in your past, you were addicted to achievement and success and climbed the corporate ladder. You are challenged to reshape what success is to you in this new stage of your life.

Since there is only 24 hours in any one day, make a conscious effort to focus on your top 10 priorities. Some examples include: health, relationship, learning, location, spirituality, hobbies, financial security, travel, being active, giving back to the community, and family.

After you have your core 10 priorities, write down what it means for you to be successful in each priority. For example, for health you could write: "Walk 3 miles every morning, attend yoga 2x weekly, and journal 4x weekly." This way you will have a measure of your success.

LEARN

You can't teach an old dog a new trick... Bullshit! Learn a new skill that you've always wanted to learn. Take up fly-fishing, birding, woodworking, basket weaving, plant identification, hiking, or walking. Maybe you already have a few solid hobbies, take them to the next level. Buy that table saw or tool that you need to take your woodworking to the next level, or a sewing machine, new rod, or GPS device. Read a book on how to further expand your skills, watch YouTube tutorials or best yet, find an apprenticeship.

WHAT TO DO

You finally made it to retirement. Talk about the ultimate hurry up and wait. For most people, lounging by the pool all day sipping on piña coladas will be awesome for about a week, then what? Besides taking up a new hobby, or building on an old one, you can seek out volunteer opportunities within the community or field of interest. See Deborah's story of how volunteering in her community changed her life in the next table.

It has become more and more common to see "retired" folks working part time or starting up businesses that they always dreamed about. Think about projects that would be fun. Look into part time opportunities helping local businesses in your area through consulting or independent contractor work.

Get connected through social networks near you, both expat and Tico. Try not to isolate into the expat world, you miss out on so much of what Costa Rica has to offer. Invite a Tico neighbor over for dinner once a month, start up or attend a "Sunday Funday" with your gringo community.

Travel and explore your new country. There are rivers, waterfalls, forest, jungles to be seen! Don't watch them on the Discovery Channel, go out and find your passion.

When in doubt, give it time. It takes time to adjust to anything new. A new schedule, a new climate, new latitude, new culture, new language, new surroundings, new activities, new expectations, and so on.

If you find yourself growing disgruntled, take a "time out" and evaluate why. If you are resenting something that is and always was Costa Rica try to change your perception and appreciate Costa Rica for what it is. Your new mantras could very well be: "I'm no longer in a rush", "Just roll with it," and "Look around, I'm in Costa Rica, who cares if the _____ takes forever!"

EXPERIENCE

Tico Angels

One reason why I love living in Costa Rica is because Tico angels appear every time you need them.

I had just dropped my partner off at the airport and was managing my way thru the roundabouts in the back road short cuts to the autopista when my clutch just died! I was stopped dead in the middle of rush hour traffic when two young boys *Tico angels* appeared on skateboards. They pushed me to a safe spot and said they were on there way to their friend's shop, and they would call a mechanic for me.

I waited about a minute and then decided it was best to find my own mechanic. I walked about a block before I heard a yell from across the street, *"BEJUCO, BEJUCO, BEJUCO."*

The angel's shop was Manuel Skate and Surf. Little did I know that I was famous to these surf/skate kids because of my filming at local beach breaks.

This was the first of many similar encounters to come. Now, whether I am in San José, Mal Pais, or Bejuco I often hear the call, "Bejuco," and I know they are talking to me.

I wish the boys knew that besides saving the day with my car they saved my life! You see, I had been floundering for awhile. I lost my career and sense of self purpose. The *Tico angels* made me realize that I had a purpose in my little beach community. I went on to start a lifeguard program selecting local surfer boys as the guards and brought in Red Cross and Coast Guard training.

In Hunington Beach I was an invisible middle aged woman, here I am infamous.

~ Deborah, *expat from CA*

HEALTHY LIVING

Kaiser recently put on a promotion geared to motivate people to lose weight through a biggest loser competition. In Costa Rica, they don't need to have competitions, why? Because they have high quality ample fruit and vegetables and casados are served in place of burgers and fries. You don't need a weight loss competition when your national dish is gallo pinto (essentially rice & beans).

Plus it's hard not to be at least a little bit active in Costa Rica. There are too many gorgeous trails and empty beaches to explore by foot!

The biggest challenge to maintaining a healthy lifestyle in Costa Rica is monitoring your alcohol intake and recreational drug use for some.

LANGUAGE BARRIER

For those of you who are fluent in Spanish, all the rest of us are jealous!

Tips for learning Spanish:

For many adults, a major factor that slows down their language acquisition is fear of making mistakes. You didn't hear this from me but, getting a slight buzz can really lubricate the tongue and ease the perfectionism in you. It can also provide the liquid bravery needed to break through your learning plateaus. Too much alcohol and you can refer back to the previous section. Picture a 3 year old learning English. They don't expect to get it all right so neither should the adult learner of a second language. They look adorable saying things wrong and you understand them. That will be you for awhile, an adorable gringo who is trying. More power to you!

LOVE LIFE

It is easy to fall into complacency, aiming at just surviving in life. Make a focused effort to rid your complacent habits and thrive, not survive! Experience each moment and appreciate what life is offering you in the now. Fall into love with life again. Just as a relationship has to be watered time and time again to keep it fresh and alive, so too does your soul and outlook on life.

If you are single in Costa Rica, there is no reason why your perfect match isn't waiting for you in the next café. I actually dated my property manager's daughter for a few years. We traveled through Costa Rica, Panama, Ecuador, and Peru! No matter what life stage you're in, it's never too late for love. My favorite Canadians met in her 50s and his 60s, married and could not be more in love! Now they each have someone to sail, kayak, paddle, explore the world, and love life with!

EXPEL THE MONSTERS

Yes, Costa Rica has robberies. Yes, Costa Rica has both good and bad people including scam artists. What country doesn't? In the US, police will respond when you call them, and will usually comply with a report and attempt to find the wrong-doer. In Costa Rica, I wouldn't say I place much faith in their "investigative work." I could choose to dwell on the worse case scenarios living in Costa Rica, but why would I do that? Who would it serve? I could do that in the States and be left with rape, murder, terrorism, and mass killings.

Worrying will only take you to the places that you fear, give you a victim's mentality, and drive away quality people. It will leave you to loneliness and potentially create a self-fulfilling prophesy.

Most Common Fears in Your Golden Years:

- You will outlive your money
- You will lose your marbles
- You will spend your last years alone

Take action with something you are passionate about as a direct rebuttal to fear. Taking action is the opposite of being a victim.

YOUR BETTER HALF

"I won't let him retire because then he'd drive me crazy!" I can't tell you how many times I have heard this from wives and husbands quoting why they can't retire. There are other options.

- Share at least one daily enthusiasm *(bird watching, cooking, volunteering, walking, swimming, kayaking, tennis, etc)*
- Let go of old arguments
- Keep yourselves in good shape
- Take responsibility for your own happiness

Recommended Books:

- *65 things to Do When You Retire*
- *The Retiring Mind*, Robert Delamontagne
- *The Couples Retirement Puzzle: 10 Must-Have Conversations for Transitioning to the Second half of Life* Robert Taylor and Dorian Mintzer

THE PART TIME EXPAT

YOU'RE NOT QUITE READY FOR THE PLUNGE BUT WOULD LIKE TO DABBLE A FOOT IN? SPECIAL CONSIDERATIONS FOR SEASONAL EXPATS

Does selling your home, your car, all of your belongings, kissing your kids and grandkids goodbye, and shipping out to Costa Rica forever sound too drastic for you? It may seem impossible for you to live far from your family.

There is a middle ground. If you are a parent or grandparent, then there is a good chance you have lived much of your life based around another's needs and desires. Now that your kids, have kids it is possible to get swallowed up into full time child care and more responsibilities than you had imagined for YOUR golden years.

The choice is yours. If you decide you are going to chase your dreams then clearly define them and see where your family fits. If living in Costa Rica full time is too much awayness, then how about 6 months out of the year? Where is your balance? How long is the flight from your family? Are there direct flights from the city where your children and grandchildren reside?

$$ LIFESTYLE

Can you have the lifestyle you desire where you currently reside on your retirement budget? If you lived in an area of Costa Rica for half of the year that was more affluent for less money would that help you fill the gap in your lifestyle goals?

Do you strive for continuity? For your six months abroad, will you want to return to Costa Rica each time or do you think you will want the freedom to explore other affordable countries in the years to come?

THE BALANCING ACT

Living in more than one location is inherently more work. There are double the utilities to turn on, off, and manage. If you rent out one or both of your homes, then you add an additional depth of complexity. Decorating, stocking, and maintaining homes in two different countries can prove exhausting. In the end, most things worth doing are difficult. Living outside the box, in two boxes rather, may be the best arrangement for you and yours.

PROPERTY MANAGEMENT

For those who opt to purchase homes, rental income can be an excellent option. Vacation rentals have allowed part-time expats to minimize costs and, in some cases, make handsome profits! Costa Rica is a tourism haven. Millions of people visit CR every year, and there is a trend towards staying in vacation rentals as opposed to hotels. This trend is why a new law *(August 5th, 2013)* will be imposed by the Costa Rica Tourism Institute (ICT). The law will require private homes and condos that are rented out as vacation rentals to pay the same taxes and fees as hotels. I'm not sure how they expect to enforce this rule on private properties. Are they going to go door to door and ask if they rent to tourists? I guess we will have to wait and see.

HOUSE-SITTERS

As homeowners you are on the flip side of those who are living rent free! You can access the same sites mentioned before in the *Living for Free* section as a homeowner seeking a house sitter. This keeps your home from attracting thieves, squatters, and keeps the house in order. Costa Rica is so humid that if the house is left unused for a period of time, rust and mold may destroy many appliances and woodwork in your home.

If you are going out of town for more than a day or two, I've had the best luck avoiding mold and musty odors by leaving the cabinets open, the ceiling fans on low, and the windows open.

If you are not comfortable using one of the services above or could not find someone on short notice, here are a few websites advertising people who make it a business to come to your house and take care of it and your pets and home.

Vicky Skinner specializes in pet massage, maintaining the pet's schedule, and will even Skype you so you can see your four-legged baby. www.lovingyourpethousesitting.com

Marita Johnson also specializes in pet and house sitting. She has numerous positive reviews. www.housepetsittercostarica.com

TRAVEL INSURANCE

If you spend no more than 6 months in one location at a time then purchasing travel insurance may be the best option for you. For more information see the *Healthcare* section.

THE MOVING BLUES

There are expats that have grown bitter and disgruntled. They focus on the wrong things. They are like salmon. They flow along with all of the excitement and arrive to fertile CR and the party is on! Shortly thereafter, they realize it is not what they thought it would be and flip a 180. They swim upstream fighting the way things are, and fighting the nature of CR that once attracted them. They are left exhausted and eventually caught, and served for dinner.

In order to have a healthy relationship, you must love your partner for exactly the person they are today with their faults, their gifts, and everything in-between. So you must appreciate CR for exactly what it is today in order to live a healthy and happy life here.

To add even more clichés, you can't live for tomorrow. Yes, some day Costa Rica might have the American consumerism you are accustomed to, but right now it doesn't. In order to be a happy resident, you must learn to appreciate what it has in the now.

I'm hopping off of my soap box now...

In every move I have made, I experienced a roller coaster of emotions. If you plan for it, it can take the edge off *a little*. Expect to have an initial high followed by an intense low. The low is mostly due to loneliness, culture shock which will be discussed next, and inaccurate expectations. Change causes stress no matter what kind of stress it is. Moving to an amazing country that fits you perfectly is still a stressful event. There are concerns you will have and worries of endless logistics: shipping your car, container, luggage, pets, new house, new area, language acquisition, new foods, access to utilities, etc.

A key method for quick acclimation is to go out and make friends in the community. Find out the inner workings of the community and how you can contribute! If you spend all day interacting with those that you left back home on Skype or magicJack then you have only left in body and are cheating your experience.

CULTURE SHOCK

This is not a phenomena that happens to the weak. It can slug you in the face or slowly tighten around you like a boa constrictor! Merriam-Webster describe culture shock as, "A sense of confusion and uncertainty sometimes with feelings of anxiety that may affect people exposed to an alien culture or environment without adequate preparation."

There are four stages of culture shock, much like grief.

- Honeymoon phase
- Negotiation phase
- Adjustment phase
- Mastery phase

Honeymoon Phase

The honeymoon phase is the high I mentioned earlier. No wrong could be done to you or by you. You are romanticized by the differences in the culture, pace, way of life, and new exotic foods. Just like the honeymoon phase in a new relationship, you are blinded to any faults of your lover's. Not until the dust settles does their obnoxious habits start to crawl under your skin, and you see the real them. When your electricity goes out in a storm, or your water gets shut off for a day or two, or when you are getting charged the wrong amount for a service and you can't get anyone to help fix it, those are some of the not-so-sexy parts of Costa Rica. Like I mentioned in the introduction: *"Costa Rica is the land of liberties, freedom, and nature. On the flip side of those liberties exist disorganization, latency, and inefficiency. The side that you choose to focus on will directly relate to your happiness and overall experience living in the pura vida, "pure life."*

Negotiation Phase

This is when reality settles in. When you sit down and wonder what have you done? All of the differences initially seen as romantic are all of the sudden cause for great concern. Can you really do this? Can you adjust to so many differences?

You realize how incredibly far away you are from "home" and your family. Maybe you don't know a soul in Costa Rica. If you aren't fluent in Spanish, that carries with it an invisible wall. While you can't see the wall, you feel it in every interaction. You feel it when you have trouble ordering meat at the butcher counter, or paying your water bill, finding the sugar in the supermarket, or asking the bus driver how much is the fare. Additionally, it is often difficult to adjust to the tropical climate (beach goers) and new bacterias in the food.

This phase is not pleasant and those who successfully navigate through it are gentle and patient with themselves. They also laugh at their mistakes, learn from others, and resolve that they are no longer in

265

a hurry and no longer in the US. They learn and adopt realistic expectations.

Adjustment Phase

During this phase, you have become accustomed to some of the new changes, like how long it takes to get your food while eating out and the long lines at the bank. You no longer fight the changes, you become accepting and build your routine around them. The changes become your new normal. Your understanding for the culture becomes more in-depth here, and you begin to cultivate connections with the community.

Mastery Phase

You feel 100% comfortable in your new culture. You accept the practices and participate in many aspects of the culture. You may not completely lose your culture of origin, but you are now an expert in the Tico way. You can navigate through any hurdle or problem as they arise knowing the appropriate course of action. You are ready to take a new expat under your wing and pass forward the experiences and knowledge that countless expats gave to you.

TIP

Remember, being an expat is not a race or a competition. It doesn't matter if you have lived in CR for 16 years, and your new friend has only been here for one. It seems like most expats want to pull out a measuring stick so they can find their place in the pecking order. Focus instead on what you have in common and enjoy each other's company.

BASIC PHRASES TO GET YOU RUNNING

START OFF "IN THE KNOW" WITH SOME HIP SLANG WORDS IN ADDITION TO
NECESSARY PHRASES WHEN MOVING ABROAD

SLANG- *Tiquismos*

- How wicked! How awesome! ¡Que mae!
- Cool- Chiva
- Cool- Tuanis
- How Boring¡Qué ahuevado!
- Really? - ¿Al chile?
- Nude, naked - A culo pelado
- To pay - Aflojar
- Unmotivated - Agachado
- Hypocrite - Agazapado
- Boring - Aguando
- To get married - Ahorcarse
- Immediately - Al tiro
- On foot - Al trole
- A passionate kiss - Aprete

Fool, ridiculous - Bañazo

A drinking binge party - Barra libre

Beer - Birra

To drink beer - Birrear

A cigarette - Blanco

To get drunk - Bombearse

An attractive woman - Bombón

Jail - Bote

Work - Brete

Boyfriend or girlfriend- Cabro

Slang for the CR city Cartago -Cartucho

One block - Cien metros

Buddy or friend - Compa

To fornicate- Coger

House - Chante

Shirt - Chema

A homosexual (insulting) -Guineo, banano, mariposa

Seriously? - ¿legal?

How bad! - ¡Qué mica!

A young person with money who dresses well - Papi

Friend - Mop

Incredible - Rajado

Wait a moment - un toque

A motorcycle - Bicha

To be stuck in traffic - Comerse la presa

A handgun - Cuete, chopo, cohete

To earn a living - Ganar la vida

Mother, or sometimes wife, lover, or a beautiful woman -Mami

To chase women - Mujerear

Your mate left you for good -Se le fue la yunta

A savior or someone who gets you out of a jam - Salvatandas

A backpack - Salveque

Literally, a 4-wheel drive vehicle. It can also be used to describe a person who is very versatile or good at many different tasks - Todo terreno

Stop fucking with me! - ¡No jodás!

Hurray up! - ¡Póngale!

Broke, no money - Tallado

RESTAURANT

The check please - la cuenta por favor

Can I have a casado with skirt steak (fish, chicken)? - Podría tener un casado con bistek (pescado, pollo)

That's all - es todo

Do you take credit cards? ¿Usted toma tarjetas?

Tap water (water of the house) - Agua de la casa

What desserts do you have? ¿Que postres tiene?

Without jalepeños - sin jalepeños

SHOPPING/ BARGAINING

How much - Cuanto cuesta

What is your best price? ¿Que is su precio meyor? -

FUELING UP

Full, diesel please - Yeno, diesel, por favor

Can you change the oil? -¿Puedes cambio el aciete?

Asking them to check the fluid levels - Liquidos tambien, por favor

PAYING THE UTILITIES

I need to pay the Electric -Nececito pagar la electricidad

- I'd like to recharge this number (Cell phone #) - Me gustaría recarga este numero
- I'd like to pay _____ account number - Me gustaría pagar cuenta numero (*account number, use for paying water bill).*

OPENING UP A NEW CELL PHONE ACCOUNT

- I need a new prepaid account for my iPhone please - Necesito una cuenta prepago nueva para mi iPhone por favor
- Yes, I do have my passport - Sí, yo tengo mi passaporte
- I'd like to put $20 on the account - me gustaría pagar vente doláres a la cuenta.

MECHANICAL PROBLEMS

- My brakes don't work - mis frenos no funcionan
- My lights don't work - Mis luces no funcionan
- Every time I hit a bump my radio turns off - cada vez que un bache mi radio se apaga
- It won't start - no se iniciará
- The battery is dead - La batería está muerta
- It makes a high pitched sound - Tiene un sonido agudo
- I ran out of gas - Me quedé sin gasolina
- The car need an oil change - El carro necesita un cambio de aceite
- Can you check the fluids? - ¿Se puede comprobar los líquidos?
- Is that part important? - ¿Es importante que los separe?
- Can you repair my tire? - ¿Se puede reparar el neumáTico?

HOUSE REPAIRS

- Screws - Tornillos
- Nails - uñas
- Hammer - martillo

- Glue - pegamento
- Plaster - yeso
- Extension chord - cuerda de extensión
- Rope - cuerda
- Chain - cadena
- Tile - azulejo
- Pipe - tubo

LOOKING FOR A PLACE TO RENT

- Does the price include utilities? - ¿El precio incluye los servicios públicos?
- Is there internet? - ¿Hay internet?
- Hot water? - Agua caliente
- Air conditioning? - Aire acondicionado
- Are there problems getting water here? - ¿Hay problemas para conseguir agua aquí?

LOOKING FOR A PLACE TO BUY

- Do you know anyone who is selling their house in the area? - ¿Conoces a alguien que está vendiendo su casa en la zona?
- Are there problems with the plumbing? - ¿Hay problemas con la fontanería?
- Is this house owner financed? - Se financia esta particular casa?
- What is the lowest price that you will take? - ¿Cuál es el precio bajo que usted tomará?
- How does the house receive water? - ¿De qué manera la casa recibe agua?

PURCHASING A CAR

How many miles are on it? - ¿Cuántas millas son en él?

What year is it? - ¿De qué año es?

When does the Riteve expire? - ¿Cuándo expira el Riteve?

Is the Placa clear? Show me - ¿Es la Placa claro? Muéstrame

What problems has the vehicle had? - ¿Qué problemas ha tenido el vehículo?

Has the car been in any accidents? - ¿El coche ha estado en algún accidente?

INTERVIEWING SCHOOLS

What is the school's accreditation? - ¿Lo que es acreditación de la escuela?-

How many students go on to attend college? - Cuántos estudiantes van a asistar a la universidad?

How much is the tuition? -¿Cuánto es la cuota?

What other expenses can we expect? - ¿Qué otros gastos se puede esperar?

What activities does the school offer?- ¿Qué actividades ofrece la escuela?

MEDICAL Spanish

I have pain in my ear - Tengo dolor en mi oído

I can't hear anything - No puedo escuchar nada

It hurts when I move my mouth - me duele cuando me muevo mi boca

My stomach hurts - Me duele el estómago

I'm allergic to Asparin - Soy alérgico a Asparin

I'm pregnant - Estoy embarazada

COOL STUFF & SERVICES

KNOWING WHERE TO GO TO BUY OR REPAIR ITEMS IS OFTEN THE
HARDEST HURDLE WHILE LIVING ABROAD

ACTIVITIES

Costa Rica Waterfall Tours
Waterfall adventures ranging from adventure seeking cliff diving, rope swinging, sliding down the falls, to a relaxing dry observation of the majestic falls.
🦶www.CostaRicaWaterfallTours.com
🦶+506-2643-1834
🦶(857) 2-GET-WET

Captain Tom's Sportfishing
Full day or half day excursions of up to 6 people all-inclusive, *beer* included!
🦶36' Custom Marcam
🦶A/C, TV, Stereo, Fighting chair
🦶www.captaintoms.com
🦶+506-2637-8994

ART

Tico POD Art House & Gifts

Decor to decorate your house with quality Costa Rican art: everything from tropical root bowls and fine ceramics to fine art pictures and original canvases.

- Website: www.fb.com/Ticopod
Telephone: + 506-2643-6090
Location: Jaco – Main Street (Calle Pastor Diaz). Located 1 building south of Surf Dogs Bar / across from Mandarina Juice.

BEAUTY

Rainforest Essences of Costa Rica
Aromatherapy, providing alternative therapeutic choices for health, beauty, and replacing chemicals with healthy oils. Awarded Sustainable award from Costa Rican Institute of Tourism.
+506-2265-7448
carpediem@ice.co.cr

BLOGS

www.costaricacurious.com
www.costaricachica.com/wordpress/
www.puravidapammy.com

CHEF
Plátano Verde
A blend of local flavor with a gourmet twist is the favorite expression of cuisine offered by Plátano Verde. They offer catering, cooking classes, private chef services, and culinary tours.
www.platanoverdecostarica.com

CPA- INTERNATIONAL

Greenback Tax Services
Provides best-in-class, expert expatriate tax services at an honest price for Americans living overseas.

CONTRACTOR

Atenas Construction
General contractor, any size job welcome. From asphalt driveways to complete homes, Guanacaste to Jaco, we'll do it right, on schedule, and on budget.
AtenasConstuction.com

CONCIERGE

Coco Concierge
Full service concierge, travel planning, tour info, and rentals. Basically, anything you need to give you more time to enjoy your life!
www.cococoncierge.com
See our Facebook Page: *Coco Concierge and Express*
www.puravidapammy.com
+506-8421-1061

CONSULTING

Your Costa Rica Advisor
Assisting you with your needs here in Costa Rica backed with 10 years of experience.
www.YourCostaRicaAdvisor.com

DOMINICAL AND SURROUNDING AREA
Chayotevine
A weekly newsletter filled with stuff for sale in the Dominical/ Perez region. Send an email to chayotevine@gmail.com to get on the list.

HOTELS/ HOSTELS

Pelicano / Pelican EStates
An adorable boutique hotel and restaurant with an adjacent property that houses 2 large private homes for rent in Esterillos Este.

Hotel Encantada
www.EncantadaCostaRica.com

A gorgeous hideaway perfect for R&R, yoga, and escaping it all. Located in Esterillos Este

10 Degrees Above
B & B in Limón that offers Photography Courses and Farm Tours.
www.10degreesabove.com
+506-8307-9218
Contact : Kimberly Beck

IMMIGRATION

Residency in Costa Rica
www.residencyincostarica.com
Javier & Maria the experts in residency. See more on pg. 58

MECHANICS

Multiservicios Montero Telephone: +506-2779-5365 Parrita, Puntarenas
Hours M-F 7am-5pm

PROPERTY SALES/ MANAGEMENT

Eco Vida
+506-8320-3354
Contact Shannon

Heredia Residential Office
Many excellent homes within your budget!
http://eltucan.co.cr/properties/

SERVICES

www.eneteenterprises.com

Enete Enterprises
Publication and business services company that publishes books in paperback and Kindle formats, writes and designs courses, and develops websites to make your passions marketable. Niche publications include: travel, guidebooks, adventure & educational courses.
www.EneteEnterprises.com

EneteEnterprises@gmail.com
619-618-0224 US

SHOPPING

Coco/ hermosa garage sale Facebook group
   To help you find things you need or sell things that you don't.

Jaco Garage Sale Facebook Group

ONLINE DIRECTORIES

- www.expat-blog.com/en/business/central-america/costa-rica/

- www.expat-blog.com/en/classifieds/central-america/costa-rica/

APN SETTINGS

Claro: Data APN: internet.ideasclaro

Móvil: Data APN: tm7datos

Movistar: Data APN: internet.movistar.cr
Data APN Username: movistarcr
Data APN Password: movistarcr

ICE: Data APN: icecelular

OUR OTHER BOOKS

Earn an Income Abroad

Becoming an Expat Ecuador

Becoming an Expat Mexico

Becoming an Expat Thailand

Becoming an Expat 101

Becoming a Nomad

Life Another Way

visit: www.Becominganexpat.com

♀to see changes in-between editions
♀for additional resources
♀to discover what we come up with next!

eLearning

If you'd like a more interactive learning experience head to www.lifeanotherway.com for our new eLearning courses complete with instructor office hours and Q&A sessions!

Editing

Lisa Bailey

Formatting

Shannon Enete

Made in the USA
Columbia, SC
27 March 2018